The
Poetry of
Louisa
May Alcott

The
Poetry of
Louisa
May Alcott

Contents

Introduction

Louisa May Alcott was born on 28 November 1832, in Germantown, now part of Philadelphia. Her father was Amos Bronson Alcott, an abolitionist, transcendentalist, and innovative, though largely unsuccessful, educator. Her mother was Abigail May, a suffragist, temperance activist, and one of the first paid social workers in the state of Massachusetts.

Her parents' involvement in various radical movements meant that the childhood of Louisa and her three sisters was unusual. She grew up surrounded by some of the period's best-known writers and thinkers, many of whom influenced her work. She wrote *Flower Fables* (1854), the first piece she published under her own name, for the daughter of Ralph Waldo Emerson and received tuition from Henry David Thoreau, who inspired one of her best poems, "Thoreau's Flute" (1863). Both writers were members of the Transcendental Club along with Bronson Alcott.

In 1843, she moved with her family to the Fruitlands in Harvard, Massachusetts, where her father made an unsuccessful attempt to establish a utopian, agrarian commune. Though it collapsed after seven months, the short-lived experience served as material for Louisa's satire *Transcendental Wild Oats* (1873). Four years later, her family acted as "station masters" for the Underground Railroad, a series of safe houses and secret routes established to aid slaves in their escape to Canada or the free states.

When the American Civil War broke out in 1861, Alcott became a volunteer nurse for the Union Army. She documented her experiences in letters sent home to her family, which were later collected, prepared for publication, and printed in *Hospital Sketches* (1863). This work was well received and won her recognition.

Alcott continued to write throughout the 1860s, producing a variety of works in different genres. These efforts included several sensational stories, such as *A Long Fatal Love Chase* (1866), published under the nom de plume A. M. Barnard. She returned to her childhood for inspiration to write the semi-autobiographical *Little Women*, which was an immediate critical and perennial commercial success upon its publication in 1868. The second volume was released a year later, followed by two sequels, *Little Men* (1871) and *Jo's Boys* (1886).

Louisa May Alcott was a prolific writer, producing an impressive array of novels, novelettes, short story collections, and plays. Though she is primarily known for her prose, she was also a fantastic poet. Her first published piece was a poem called "Sunlight," printed under the name Flora Fairfield in 1851, and she continued to publish poems throughout her illustrious career. Her poetry is as varied as the rest of her writing, addressing a range of topics and audiences. She died of a stroke on 6 March 1888, two days after the death of her father.

Sleep, Little Seed

Sleep, little seed,
Deep in your bed,
While winter snow
Lies overhead.
Wake, little sprout,
And drink the rain,
Till sunshine calls
You to rise again
Strike deep, young root,
In the earth below;
Unfold, pale leaves,
Begin to grow.
Baby bud, dance
In the warm sun;
Bloom, sweet rose,
Life has begun.

Fairy Song

The moonlight fades from flower and rose
    And the stars dim one by one;
The tale is told, the song is sung,
    And the Fairy feast is done.
The night-wind rocks the sleeping flowers,
    And sings to them, soft and low.
The early birds erelong will wake:
    'Tis time for the Elves to go.

O'er the sleeping earth we silently pass,
    Unseen by mortal eye,
And send sweet dreams, as we lightly float
    Through the quiet moonlit sky;—
For the stars' soft eyes alone may see,
    And the flowers alone may know,
The feasts we hold, the tales we tell;
    So 'tis time for the Elves to go.

From bird, and blossom, and bee,
    We learn the lessons they teach;
And seek, by kindly deeds, to win
    A loving friend in each.
And though unseen on earth we dwell,
    Sweet voices whisper low,
And gentle hearts most joyously greet
    The Elves where'er they go.

When next we meet in the Fairy dell,
    May the silver moon's soft light
Shine then on faces gay as now,

And Elfin hearts as light.
Now spread each wing, for the eastern sky
    With sunlight soon shall glow.
The morning star shall light us home:
    Farewell! for the Elves must go.

Flowers, Dear Flowers, Farewell!

We are sending you, dear flowers
    Forth alone to die,
Where your gentle sisters may not weep
    O'er the cold graves where you lie;
But you go to bring them fadeless life
    In the bright homes where they dwell,
And you softly smile that 'tis so,
    As we sadly sing farewell.

O plead with gentle words for us,
    And whisper tenderly
Of generous love to that cold heart,
    And it will answer ye;
And though you fade in a dreary home,
    Yet loving hearts will tell
Of the joy and peace that you have given:
    Flowers, dear flowers, farewell!

Brighter Shone the Golden Shadows

Brighter shone the golden shadows;
    On the cool wind softly came
The low, sweet tones of happy flowers,
    Singing little Violet's name.
'Mong the green trees was it whispered,
    And the bright waves bore it on
To the lonely forest flowers,
    Where the glad news had not gone.

Thus the Frost-King lost his kingdom,
    And his power to harm and blight.
Violet conquered, and his cold heart
    Warmed with music, love, and light;
And his fair home, once so dreary,
    Gay with lovely Elves and flowers,
Brought a joy that never faded
    Through the long bright summer hours.

Thus, by Violet's magic power,
    All dark shadows passed away,
And on the home of happy flowers
    The golden light for ever lay.
Thus the Fairy mission ended,
    And all Flower-Land was taught
The "Power of Love," by gentle deeds
    That little Violet wrought.

Hither, Hither

Hither, hither, from thy home,
Airy sprite, I bid thee come!
Born of roses, fed on dew,
Charms and potions canst thou brew?
Bring me here, with elfin speed,
The fragrant philter which I need.
Make it sweet and swift and strong,
Spirit, answer now my song!

* * * * *

Hither I come,
From my airy home,
Afar in the silver moon.
Take the magic spell,
And use it well,
Or its power will vanish soon!

Oh When Thy Heart Is Full of Fears

Oh when thy heart is full of fears
And the way is dim to Heaven
When the sorrow and the sin of years
Peace from thy soul has driven
Then through the mist of falling tears
Look up and be forgiven.

And then rise up and sin no more
And from thy dark ways flee
Let Virtue o'er thy appetites
Have full and perfect mastery
And the kindly ones that hover o'er
Will ever strengthen thee.

And though thou art helpless and forlorn
Let not thy heart's peace go
And though the riches of this world are gone
And thy lot is care and woe
Faint not, but journey ever on
True wealth is not below.

Oh, falter not but still look up
Let Patience be thy guide
Bless the rod and take the cup
And trustfully abide
Let not temptation vanquish thee
And the Father will provide.

An Advertisement

Ho! all ye nervous women folk,
Who sigh that you were born;
Come, try a sovereign remedy
For half the ills you mourn.
I lately have discovered it,
And proved its potency,
By tasting at the fountain-head—
Tremont Place, Number Three.

Here, at this moral restaurant,
Our sex may always find,
When weary of domestic stews,
Nice lunches for the mind.
Essays are served at certain hours,
Gossip, of course, is free;
Discussion always is on tap,
And once a month, Club Tea.

I know whereof I speak, my friends,
For at this Woman's Club
I found a pleasant mingling
Of Heaven and the Hub.
No wine, cigars or gambling,
But wisdom, wit, and fun,
The matrons knit their husband's hose,
And quoted Emerson.

Wise virgins had their lamps well trimmed,
And lighted up the rooms
With luster of brave words and deeds,—

Worthy the noblest grooms;
Yet strong enough to stand alone,
(In hygienic boots),
And bear life's burdens, for they wore
The famous "freedom suits."

"Home" was the dish we feasted on,
The evening I was there;
Garnished with eloquence, and served
On finest Cheney ware,
Porter was sipped to soothe the brains
Beneath each lofty bonnet;
No pewter pot the liquor held,
But it had a good "head" on it.

Flowers were there, and one I saw
That bore an honored name;
In Boston it has flourished long,
And with the Pilgrims came.
This plant a worthy scion was,
Stately and strong and gay;
'Twill make the modest posy blush
To add, it blooms in May.

Among the hills the farmers think
The Peabody bird sings ever,
"Sow your wheat! sow your wheat!" as if
To rouse all to endeavor.
Two Peabody birds this Club possessed.
One did cheerily sing
"We've gained our seats at last!" and one
"Let Kindergartens spring!"

I looked about me for the queen
Who ruled this busy hive,
Where work and play, reform and fun,
Together seemed to thrive.
I said, "I wish their magic spell
These blithe souls would avow."
A dozen voices answered me—
"Look round and you'll see Howe."

I said, "Can strangers enter here,
Led by some friendly Star?"
They answered, "If their Ames be good,
We care not who they are;
The young, the old, the rich, the poor,
And if a noble male
We Ferrette out, we welcome him,
With 'Worthy brother, Hale!'"

Then hasten, all ye women folk:
Tuck up your skirts and walk.
Here's food for hungry hearts and souls,
Here mind with mind may talk.
Here spirits of the best are found,
Here flows the true Club Tea,
And the cream of human kindness,
At Tremont Place, Number Three.

"The Rose Family" Song I

O flower at my window
    Why blossom you so fair,
With your green and purple cup
    Upturned to sun and air?
"I bloom, blithesome Bessie,
    To cheer your childish heart;
The world is full of labor,
    And this shall be my part."
            Whirl, busy wheel, faster,
                Spin, little thread, spin;
            The sun shines fair without,
                And we are gay within.

O robin in the tree-top,
    With sunshine on your breast,
Why brood you so patiently
    Above your hidden nest?
"I brood, blithesome Bessie,
    And sing my humble song,
That the world may have more music
    From my little ones erelong."
            Whirl, busy wheel, faster,
                Spin, little thread, spin;
            The sun shines fair without,
                And we are gay within.

O balmy wind of summer,
    O silver-singing brook,
Why rustle through the branches?
    Why shimmer in your nook?

"I flutter, blithesome Bessie,
    Like a blessing far and wide;
I scatter bloom and verdure
    Where'er my footsteps glide."
        Whirl, busy wheel, faster,
            Spin, little thread, spin;
        The sun shines fair without,
            And we are gay within.

O brook and breeze and blossom,
    And robin on the tree,
You make a joy of duty,
    A pride of industry;
Teach me to work as blithely,
    With a willing hand and heart:
The world is full of labor,
    And I must do my part.
        Whirl, busy wheel, faster,
            Spin, little thread, spin;
        The sun shines fair without,
            And we are gay within.

"The Rose Family" Song II

O lesson well and wisely taught
    Stay with me to the last,
That all my life may better be
    For the trial that is past.
O vanity, mislead no more!
    Sleep, like passions, long!
Wake, happy heart, and dance again
    To the music of my song!

O summer days, flit fast away,
    And bring the blithesome hour
When we three wanderers shall meet
    Safe in our household flower!
O dear mamma, lament no more!
    Smile on us as we come,
Your grief has been our punishment,
    Your love has led us home.

Cold Winds May Blow

Cold winds may blow,
    And snows may fall,
But well we know
    God cares for all.

I Wish I Had a Quiet Tomb

I wish I had a quiet tomb,
    Beside a little rill;
Where birds, and bees, and butterflies,
    Would sing upon the hill.

Brindle and Bess

Brindle and Bess,
White-star and Jess—
    Come, butter, come!
Eat cowslips fine,
Red columbine—
    Come, butter, come!
Grasses, green and tall,
Clover, best of all,—
    Come, butter, come!
And give every night
Milk sweet and white—
    Come, butter, come!
Make the churn go.
See the lumps grow!—
    Come, butter, come!

A Song for Little Freddie on His Third Birthday

Down in the field
Where the brook goes,
Lives a white lammie
With a little black nose.

He eats the grass so green,
He drinks the "la la" sweet,

"Buttertupts" and daisies,
Grow all about his feet.

The "birdies" they sing to him,
The big sun in the sky,
Warms his little "Toe-toes,"
And peeps into his eye.

He's a very gentle lammie,
He never makes a fuss,
He never "saps his marmar,"
He never says "I muss."

He hops and he runs,
"Wound and wound" all day,
And when the night comes,
He goes "bye low" on the hay.

In a nice little barn,
Where the "moo-moos" are;
Freddie says "Good night,"
But the lammie he says "Baa!"

A Song for a Christmas Tree

Cold and wintry is the sky,
Bitter winds go whistling by,
Orchard boughs are bare and dry,
Yet here stands a fruitful tree.
Household fairies kind and dear,
With loving magic none need fear,
Bade it rise and blossom here,
Little friends, for you and me.

Come and gather as they fall,
Shining gifts for great and small;
Santa Claus remembers all
When he comes with goodies piled.
Corn and candy, apples red,
Sugar horses, gingerbread,
Babies who are never fed,
Are hanging here for every child.

Shake the boughs and down they come,
Better fruit than peach or plum,
'Tis our little harvest home;
For though frosts the flowers kill,
Though birds depart and squirrels sleep,
Though snows may gather cold and deep,
Little folk their sunshine keep,
And mother-love makes summer still.

Gathered in a smiling ring,
Lightly dance and gayly sing,
Still at heart remembering

The sweet story all should know,
    Of the little Child whose birth
    Has made this day throughout the earth
    A festival for childish mirth,
Since that first Christmas long ago.

In the Garret

Four little chests all in a row,
    Dim with dust, and worn by time,
All fashioned and filled, long ago,
    By children now in their prime.
Four little keys hung side by side,
    With faded ribbons, brave and gay
When fastened there, with childish pride,
    Long ago, on a rainy day.
Four little names, one on each lid,
    Carved out by a boyish hand,
And underneath there lieth hid
    Histories of the happy band
Once playing here, and pausing oft
    To hear the sweet refrain,
That came and went on the roof aloft,
    In the falling summer rain.

"Meg" on the first lid, smooth and fair.
    I look in with loving eyes,
For folded here, with well-known care,

A goodly gathering lies—
The record of a peaceful life,
 Gifts to gentle child and girl,
A bridal gown, lines to a wife,
 A tiny shoe, a baby curl.
No toys in this first chest remain,
 For all are carried away,
In their old age, to join again
 In another small Meg's play.
Ah, happy mother! Well I know
 You hear, like a sweet refrain,
Lullabies ever soft and low
 In the falling summer rain.

"Jo" on the next lid, scratched and worn,
 And within a motley store
Of headless dolls, of schoolbooks torn,
 Birds and beasts that speak no more,
Spoils brought home from the fairy ground
 Only trod by youthful feet,
Dreams of a future never found,
 Memories of a past still sweet,
Half-writ poems, stories wild,
 April letters, warm and cold,
Diaries of a wilful child,
 Hints of a woman early old,
A woman in a lonely home,
 Hearing, like a sad refrain—
"Be worthy, love, and love will come,"
 In the falling summer rain.

My Beth! the dust is always swept
　　From the lid that bears your name,
As if by loving eyes that wept,
　　By careful hands that often came.
Death canonized for us one saint,
　　Ever less human than divine,
And still we lay, with tender plaint,
　　Relics in this household shrine—
The silver bell, so seldom rung,
　　The little cap which last she wore,
The fair, dead Catherine that hung
　　By angels borne above her door.
The songs she sang, without lament,
　　In her prison-house of pain,
Forever are they sweetly blent
　　With the falling summer rain.

Upon the last lid's polished field—
　　Legend now both fair and true
A gallant knight bears on his shield,
　　"Amy" in letters gold and blue.
Within lie snoods that bound her hair,
　　Slippers that have danced their last,
Faded flowers laid by with care,
　　Fans whose airy toils are past,
Gay valentines, all ardent flames,
　　Trifles that have borne their part
In girlish hopes and fears and shames,
　　The record of a maiden heart
Now learning fairer, truer spells,

Hearing, like a blithe refrain,
The silver sound of bridal bells
    In the falling summer rain.

Four little chests all in a row,
    Dim with dust, and worn by time,
Four women, taught by weal and woe
    To love and labor in their prime.
Four sisters, parted for an hour,
    None lost, one only gone before,
Made by love's immortal power,
    Nearest and dearest evermore.
Oh, when these hidden stores of ours
    Lie open to the Father's sight,
May they be rich in golden hours,
    Deeds that show fairer for the light,
Lives whose brave music long shall ring,
    Like a spirit-stirring strain,
Souls that shall gladly soar and sing
    In the long sunshine, after rain.

My Pretty Little Mermaid

My pretty little mermaid,
    Oh! come, and play with me:
I'll love you, I'll welcome you;
    And happy we shall be.

Hebe Poured the Nectar Forth

Hebe poured the nectar forth
    When gods of old were jolly,
But graces three our goblets fill,
    Fair Portia, Pris and Polly.
Their draughts make every man who tastes
    Happier, better, richer;
So here we vow ourselves henceforth
    Knights of the Silver Pitcher.

An Autumn Song

Autumn skies are cold and gloomy,
Mournful winds begin to sigh,
Withered leaves float slowly downward,
Lingering flowers fade and die;
Nature's summer work is over,
Her rich harvests garnered lie,
And she rests content and grateful,
Heedless of the sombre sky.
Trusting in the future spring-time,
Greeting winter without fear,
Musing gladly o'er past labors,
In the twilight of the year;
While her cheerful heart finds music
In the melancholy wind,
And the thought of summer lingers
Like a sunbeam left behind.

The autumn of your life, mother,
Brings its shadow to your sky,
Cherished hopes like pale leaves wither,
Memories like sad winds sigh.
Now your summer work is over;
Time's frosts your flowers kill;
But the store-house of the future
Richest harvests surely fill.
Lone enduring, brave endeavor,
Through long years of care and strife,
Bring their sweet reward to comfort
All the twilight hours of life.
There can fall no snow of winter,

There can blow no bitter wind,
Where such memories warmly linger
Like a sunbeam left behind.

Mary's Dream

The moon had climbed the eastern hill
    Which rises o'er the sands of Dee,
And from its highest summit shed
    A silver light on tower and tree,
When Mary laid her down to sleep
    (Her thoughts on Sandy far at sea);
When soft and low a voice was heard,
    Saying, "Mary, weep no more for me."

She from her pillow gently raised
    Her head, to see who there might be,
And saw young Sandy, shivering, stand
    With visage pale and hollow e'e.
    "Oh Mary dear, cold is my clay;
    It lies beneath the stormy sea;
Far, far from thee, I sleep in death.
    Dear Mary, weep no more for me.

    "Three stormy nights and stormy days
    We tossed upon the raging main.
And long we strove our bark to save;
    But all our striving was in vain.

E'en then, when terror chilled my blood,
　　My heart was filled with love of thee.
The storm is past, and I'm at rest;
　　So, Mary, weep no more for me.

　　"Oh maiden dear, yourself prepare;
　　We soon shall meet upon that shore
Where love is free from doubt and care,
　　And you and I shall part no more."
Loud crew the cock, the shadow fled;
　　No more her Sandy did she see;
But soft the passing spirit said,
　　　"Sweet Mary, weep no more for me."

Oh My Heart Is Sad and Weary

Oh my heart is sad and weary
    Everywhere I roam,
Longing for the old plantation
    And for the old folks at home.

But I'll Be Contented

But I'll be contented
    With what I have got;
Of folly repented,
    Then sweet is my lot.

Oh, Peggy Was a Jolly Lass

Oh, Peggy was a jolly lass,
    Ye heave ho, boys, ye heave ho!
She never grudged her Jack a glass,
    Ye heave ho, boys, ye heave ho!
And when he sailed the raging main,
She faithful was unto her swain,
    Ye heave ho, boys, ye heave ho!

Here Lies the Bravest Cock That Ever Crew

Here lies the bravest cock that ever crew:
We mourn for him with sorrow true.
Now nevermore at dawn his music shall we hear,
Waking the world like trumpet shrill and clear.
The hens all hang their heads, the chickens sadly peep;
The boys look sober, and the girls all weep.
Good-by, dear Cocky: sleep and rest,
With grass and daisies on your faithful breast;
And when you wake, brave bird, so good and true,
Clap your white wings and crow, "Cock-a-doodle-doo."

Despondency

Silent and sad,
When all are glad,
And the earth is dressed in flowers;
When the gay birds sing
Till the forests ring,
As they rest in woodland bowers.

Oh, why these tears,
And these idle fears
For what may come to-morrow?
The birds find food
From God so good,
And the flowers know no sorrow.

If He clothes these
And the leafy trees,
Will He not cherish thee?
Why doubt His care;
It is everywhere,
Though the way we may not see.

Then why be sad
When all are glad,
And the world is full of flowers?
With the gay birds sing,
Make life all Spring,
And smile through the darkest hours.

A. B. A

Like Bunyan's pilgrim with his pack,
　　Forth went the dreaming youth
To seek, to find, and make his own
　　Wisdom, virtue, and truth.
Life was his book, and patiently
　　He studied each hard page;
By turns reformer, outcast, priest,
　　Philosopher and sage.

Christ was his Master, and he made
　　His life a gospel sweet;
Plato and Pythagoras in him
　　Found a disciple meet.
The noblest and best his friends,
　　Faithful and fond, though few;
Eager to listen, learn, and pay
　　The love and honor due.

Power and place, silver and gold,
　　He neither asked nor sought;
Only to serve his fellowmen,
　　With heart and word and thought.
A pilgrim still, but in his pack
　　No sins to frighten or oppress;
But wisdom, morals, piety,
　　To teach, to warn and bless.

The world passed by, nor cared to take
　　The treasure he could give;
Apart he sat, content to wait

And beautifully live;
Unsaddened by long, lonely years
    Of want, neglect, and wrong,
His soul to him a kingdom was,
    Steadfast, serene, and strong.

Magnanimous and pure his life,
    Tranquil its happy end;
Patience and peace his handmaids were,
    Death an immortal friend.
For him no monuments need rise,
    No laurels make his pall;
The mem'ry of the good and wise
    Outshines, outlives them all.

A Song from the Suds

Queen of my tub, I merrily sing,
    While the white foam raises high,
And sturdily wash, and rinse, and wring,
    And fasten the clothes to dry;
Then out in the free fresh air they swing,
    Under the sunny sky.

I wish we could wash from our hearts and our souls
    The stains of the week away,
And let water and air by their magic make
    Ourselves as pure as they;
Then on the earth there would be indeed
    A glorious washing-day!

Along the path of a useful life
    Will heart's-ease ever bloom;
The busy mind has no time to think
    Of sorrow, or care, or gloom;
And anxious thoughts may be swept away
    As we busily wield a broom.

I am glad a task to me is given
    To labor at day by day;
For it brings me health, and strength, and hope,
    And I cheerfully learn to say—
"Head, you may think; heart, you may feel;
    But hand, you shall work alway!"

Fairy Firefly

Child

O Firefly! I have caught you fast:
    Don't flutter in a rage;
But shine for me a little while
    Here in this dainty cage.
Why are you wandering so late,
    With your small lamp alight,
When bird and bee and butterfly
    Are sleeping through the night?
Come, tell to me a fairy tale;
    Amuse me while you stay;
And, when it's time to go to bed,
    You shall safely fly away.

Firefly

I'll tell my own sad story, child,
    Here shining in your net;
And, though I fly away so soon,
    I pray you, don't forget:—
I was a lovely fairy once,
    Blithe as an early lark;
And in my little bosom shone
    A beautiful, bright spark:
That was my elfin spirit, dear;
    And, while I lived aright,
It was to me a guiding star,
    To lead me to the light.
I should have loved the blessèd sun,

And tried to follow him;
But, no, I turned my face away,
    And my bright spark grew dim.
My daily duties were not done;
    I did not tend the flowers;
I did not help the honey-bees
    Improve their shining hours;
No baby butterfly I taught
    To spread its tender wing;
No young bird ever learned of me
    The airy songs we sing.
I left my playmates, one and all,
    So innocent, so gay,—
I would not listen to their words,
    But coldly turned away.
All day I slept, with folded wings,
    Lulled by the singing brook,
Where tall ferns made a shady tent,
    And guarded my still nook.
But, when the stars came out, I woke;
    I loved the meadows damp;
I liked to hear the cricket sing;
    To watch the glow-worm's lamp,
The round-eyed owl, and beetle fierce,
    The hungry, buzzing gnat,
The giddy moth, the croaking frog,
    And stealthy-wingèd bat.
These were the friends I freely chose,
    These, and the primrose pale;
I did not even seek to know
    A star or nightingale.
I turned away from lovely things,

I revelled in the dark,
And day by day more faintly shone
        My precious bosom-spark,
Until, at last, it came to be
        This feeble, fitful light,
And my dim eyes no power had
        To see, except by night.
My fairy form passed quite away;
        Alas! I'd gladly die,
For 'tis my punishment to be
        A wandering firefly.
Ah! now I long for all I've lost:
        My mates are flown away;
The birds and bees I pine to see,
        But cannot seek by day.
I haunt the flowers all the night,
        Hoping a home to win,—
The doors are shut: all are asleep:
        I knock; none let me in.
I'm tired of the friends I made;
        I hate the teasing gnat,
The hooting owl, the cricket shrill,
        The beetle, and the bat.
My only mates are the poor moths;
        They seek and love the light,
Though they, like me, sleep all day long,
        And only fly by night.
Once they were butterflies, you know,
        And floated in the sun;
But they are doomed to expiate
        The wrongs which they have done,
By madly longing for the shine

That blinds their feeble eye,
Yet draws them, like a dreadful spell,
    To flutter, burn, and die.
O little child! be warned in time;
    Guard well your bosom-spark,
Else it will slowly fade away,
    And leave you in the dark.
Feed it with all things fair and good:
Then gloomy clouds may roll,
But cannot shadow in your life,—
    'Tis sunshine of the soul.

A Little Grey Curl

A little grey curl from my father's head
    I find unburned on the hearth,
And give it a place in my diary here,
    With a feeling half sadness, half mirth.
For the long white locks are our special pride,
    Though he smiles at his daughter's praise;
But, oh, they have grown each year more thin,
    Till they are now but a silvery haze.

That wise old head! (though it does grow bald
    With the knocks hard fortune may give)
Has a store of faith and hope and trust,
    Which have taught him how to live.
Though the hat be old, there's a face below
    Which telleth to those who look
The history of a good man's life,
    And it cheers like a blessed book.

A peddler of jewels, of clocks, and of books,
    Many a year of his wandering youth;
A peddler still, with a far richer pack,
    His wares are wisdom and love and truth.
But now, as then, few purchase or pause,
    For he cannot learn the tricks of trade;
Little silver he wins, but that which time
    Is sprinkling thick on his meek old head.

But there'll come a day when the busy world,
    Grown sick with its folly and pride,
Will remember the mild-faced peddler then

Whom it rudely had set aside;
Will remember the wares he offered it once
 And will seek to find him again,
Eager to purchase truth, wisdom, and love,
 But, oh, it will seek him in vain.

It will find but his footsteps left behind
 Along the byways of life,
Where he patiently walked, striving the while
 To quiet its tumult and strife.
But the peddling pilgrim has laid down his pack
 And gone with his earnings away;
How small will they seem, remembering the debt
 Which the world too late would repay.

God bless the dear head! and crown it with years
 Untroubled and calmly serene;
That the autumn of life more golden may be
 For the heats and the storms that have been.
My heritage none can ever dispute,
 My fortune will bring neither strife nor care;
'Tis an honest name, 'tis a beautiful life,
 And the silver lock of my father's hair.

Beds to the Front of Them

Beds to the front of them,
Beds to the right of them,
Beds to the left of them,
    Nobody blundered.
Beamed at by hungry souls,
Screamed at with brimming bowls,
Steamed at by army rolls,
    Buttered and sundered.
With coffee not cannon plied,
Each must be satisfied,
Whether they lived or died;
    All the men wondered.

Faith

Oh, when the heart is full of fears
    And the way seems dim to heaven,
When the sorrow and the care of years
    Peace from the heart has driven,—
Then, through the mist of falling tears,
    Look up and be forgiven.

Forgiven for the lack of faith
    That made all dark to thee,
Let conscience o'er thy wayward soul
    Have fullest mastery:
Hope on, fight on, and thou shalt win
    A noble victory.

Though thou art weary and forlorn,
    Let not thy heart's peace go;
Though the riches of this world are gone,
    And thy lot is care and woe,
Faint not, but journey hourly on:
    True wealth is not below.

Through all the darkness still look up:
    Let virtue be thy guide;
Take thy draught from sorrow's cup,
    Yet trustfully abide;
Let not temptation vanquish thee,
    And the Father will provide.

God Comfort Thee Dear Mother

God comfort thee dear mother,
For sorrow sad and deep
Is lying heavy on thy heart
And this hath made thee weep.

There is a Father o'er us, mother,
Who orders for the best
And peace shall come ere long, mother,
And dwell within thy breast.

Then let us journey onward, mother,
And trustfully abide,
The coming forth of good or ill
Whatever may betide.

Fragment from "The Mysterious Key and What it Opened"

Love comes to all soon or late,
And maketh gay or sad;
For every bird will find its mate,
And every lass a lad.

French Song

J'avais une colombe blanche,
J'avais un blanc petit pigeon,
Tous deux volaient, de branche en branche,
Jusqu'au faîte de mon dongeon:
Mais comme un coup de vent d'automne,
S'est abattu là, l'épervier,
Et ma colombe si mignonne
Ne revient plus au colombier.

Fragments from *Under the Lilacs*

So he took up his bow,
And he feathered his arrow,
And said, "I will shoot
This little cock-sparrow."

* * * * *

Benny had a little dog,
His fleece was white as snow,
And everywhere that Benny went,
The dog was sure to go.

He went into the School one day,
which was against the rule;
It made the children laugh and play
To see a dog—

From Our Happy Home

From our happy home
Through the world we roam
One week in all the year,
Making winter spring
With the joy we bring
For Christmas-tide is here.

Now the eastern star
Shines from afar
To light the poorest home;
Hearts warmer grow,
Gifts freely flow,
For Christmas-tide has come.

Now gay trees rise
Before young eyes,
Abloom with tempting cheer;
Blithe voices sing,
And blithe bells ring,
For Christmas-tide is here.

Oh, happy chime,
Oh, blessèd time,
That draws us all so near!
"Welcome, dear day,"
All creatures say,
For Christmas-tide is here.

Gingerbread

Gingerbread,
Go to the head.
Your task is done;
A soul is won.
Take it and go
Where muffins grow,
Where sweet loaves rise
To the very skies,
And biscuits fair
Perfume the air.
Away, away!
Make no delay;
In the sea of flour
Plunge this hour.
Safe in your breast
Let the yeast-cake rest,
Till you rise in joy,
A white bread boy!

The Patient Drop

"It's very lonely here,"
Sighed a shining little drop.
"I wish the busy waves
Would ever choose to stop.
I lie idle in this shell,
Rocking to and fro,
I should dearly love to join
The ocean in its flow.
But I will not sigh and murmur,
But be of better cheer
And try to find some pleasure
While lying lonely here."
A warm-hearted sunbeam,
Glancing brightly by,
Heard the whisper of the drop
And listened to its sigh,
And thought within itself,
"I will reward it well,
And soon in a pleasant home
The patient drop shall dwell."
So when the mists arose
From the bosom of the sea,
From its prison in the shell
The little drop was free.
For the sunbeam drew it up
And left it in the sky,
Where dark and gloomy clouds
Were swiftly rolling by.
"Alas," said the little drop,
"Where shall I go?

All is strange above here,
I dare not look below.
Never mind, I'll be brave,
And banish all my fear,
The sun is in the heavens
And soon will appear."
So patiently it stayed
In the stormy troubled sky,
Till other little drops
Came gaily hastening by.
"Oh come with us," they cried,
"And join in our play,
We can dance and frolic now,
'Tis to be a rainy day."
Then away went they all
From their cloudy home on high,
And merry games they played
Falling from the sky;
Some pattered on the house-tops,
Some tapped on the pane,
Calling to the children
To come and watch the rain;
Some fell in people's faces,
Taking roguish care
To drop upon their noses,
Or light among their hair;
Some splashed in the pools,
With a tinkle low and sweet,
Where the downy little ducklings
Bathed their yellow feet;
Some wet the quiet cattle
Drinking at the springs,

Causing them to wonder
At the ever-spreading rings.
Some went into the fields
Where corn was tall and green,
And washed the rosy faces
Of the poppies in between.
Some stole into the forest,
Rustling on the ground
All among the withered leaves
With a pleasant sound;
Filling empty acorn cups,
Lying far and near,
That the elves might find them
Full of water clear.
Some dashed into the ocean,
To swell its busy flow;
Some sank, to change ere long
Into precious pearls below.
But the patient little drop
Went on with many more,
Far away from the sound
Of the sea and its roar.
They went into the garden,
Where all the thirsty flowers
Danced upon their stems
To see the welcome showers;
And the drops all gladly fell
Into their bosoms fair,
Content to leave their play
And rest forever there.
But the little drop we follow
Sank deep into the ground,

And in its quiet bosom
A resting place it found.
"Ah! this is stranger far
Than sea shore or sky,
In what a dreary place
I have now come to lie.
Still, I'll keep a brave heart,
Something good will come,
And I at last may find
A quiet happy home."
A little sprout hard by,
Wrapped in dusky skin,
Saw the lovely drop there
And softly sucked it in,
Saying "If you strengthen me,
Who am small and weak,
I will bear you upward
Into the light you seek."
So together they rose daily
Till they reached the upper air,
And there the plant blossomed,
A flower fresh and fair.
And the drop, forgetting self,
Of the plant became a part,
And found a pleasant home
In the lily's golden heart.
Then the sunbeam smiling said,
"I have tried your patience well,
Now here, with the lily queen,
I'll leave you to dwell.
Be ever as patient, Drop,
And round you will play

The sunlight of happiness
That will never fade away."

⚜

I Write About the Butterfly

I write about the butterfly,
    It is a pretty thing;
And flies about like the birds,
    But it does not sing.

First it is a little grub,
    And then it is a nice yellow cocoon,
And then the butterfly
    Eats its way out soon.

They live on dew and honey,
    They do not have any hive,
They do not sting like wasps, and bees, and hornets,
    And to be as good as they are we should strive.

Summer Days are Over

Summer days are over,
    Summer work is done;
Harvests have been gathered
    Gayly one by one.
Now the feast is eaten,
    Finished is the play;
But one rite remains for
    Our Thanksgiving-day.

Best of all the harvest
    In the dear God's sight,
Are the happy children
    In the home to-night;
And we come to offer
    Thanks where thanks are due,
With grateful hearts and voices,
    Father, mother, unto you.

Little Shadows, Little Shadows

Little shadows, little shadows
    Dancing on the chamber wall,
While I sit beside the hearthstone
    Where the red flames rise and fall.
Caps and nightgowns, caps and nightgowns,
    My three antic shadows wear;
And no sound they make in playing,
    For the six small feet are bare.

Dancing gayly, dancing gayly,
    To and fro all together,
Like a family of daisies
    Blown about in windy weather;
Nimble fairies, nimble fairies,
    Playing pranks in the warm glow,
While I sing the nursery ditties
    Childish phantoms love and know.

Now what happens, now what happens?
    One small shadow's tumbled down:
I can see it on the carpet
    Softly rubbing its hurt crown.
No one whimpers, no one whimpers;
    A brave-hearted sprite is this:
See! the others offer comfort
    In a silent, shadowy kiss.

Hush! they're creeping; hush! they're creeping,
    Up about my rocking-chair:
I can feel their loving fingers

Clasp my neck and touch my hair.
Little shadows, little shadows,
    Take me captive, hold me tight,
As they climb and cling and whisper,
    "Mother dear, good night! good night!"

***

Swallow, Swallow, Neighbor Swallow

    Swallow, swallow, neighbor swallow,
        Starting on your autumn flight,
Pause a moment at my window,
        Twitter softly your good-night;
For the summer days are over,
        All your duties are well done,
And the happy homes you builded
        Have grown empty, one by one.

    Swallow, swallow, neighbor swallow,
        Are you ready for your flight?
Are all the feather cloaks completed?
        Are the little caps all right?
Are the young wings strong and steady
        For the journey through the sky?
Come again in early spring-time;
        And till then, good-by, good-by!

Give Me a Freshening Breeze, My Boys

Give me a freshening breeze, my boys,
    A white and swelling sail,
A ship that cuts the dashing waves,
    And weathers every gale.
What life is like a sailor's life,
    So free, so bold, so brave?
His home the ocean's wide expanse,
    A coral bed his grave.

And if Your Nancy Frowns, My Lad

And if your Nancy frowns, my lad,
And scorns a jacket blue,
Just hoist your sails for other ports,
And find a maid more true.

Goldfin and Silvertail

Little Bessie lay in a rocky nook,
    Alone, beside the sea,
Where the sound of ever-rolling waves
    To her ear came pleasantly.
Her face was dark with a gloomy frown,
    Tears on her hot cheek lay;
For a wilful, unkind little girl
    She had been that livelong day;
And had stolen here, to the quiet shore,
    To sigh and sob alone,
And to wonder how and why and where
    Her happiness all had flown.
As thus she lay, with half-closed eyes,
    Low voices reached her ear,
And laughter gay that seemed to flow
    Like ripples sweet and clear.
She looked above, she looked below
    And saw with wondering glee
Two little mermaids on the rocks,
    Both singing merrily.
One combed her long and shining hair,
    All wreathed with sea-weed bright;
The other caught the falling spray
    That leaped into the light.
Friendly and fair both faces seemed,
    With smiling lips and eyes,
And little arms and bosoms white
    As sea-foam when it flies.
But Bessie wondered more and more,
    And Bessie's cheek grew pale;

For both the mermaids bore below
        A graceful little tail,—
One, bright with silver scales, that shone
        In every fin and fold;
The other, brighter, stranger still,
        All glittering with gold.
"Come hither, little mermaids, pray,"
        Cried Bessie, from her nook,
"I will not touch or trouble you,—
        I only want to look."
The startled mermaids glanced at her,
        And whispered long and low;
At last, one to the other said,
        "Dear Goldfin, let us go."
Then, gliding from their rocky seat,
        And floating through the sea,
They reached the nook where Bessie lay,
        And looked up smilingly:
"Now, ask of us whate'er you will,
        We'll surely grant it thee,"
Bright Goldfin said unto the child,
        Who watched them silently.
And Bessie answered with delight,
        "You seem so blithe and gay,
And I'm so sad and lonely here,
        Make me a mermaid, pray."
" Ah! choose again: that is not wise,"
        Cried Goldfin, earnestly;
"I have no spell to change your heart,
        And sadder it may be.
Our home is strange and wild to you;
        Think what you leave behind,—

Sunshine and home, and, best of all,
    A mother, dear and kind."
But Bessie only frowned and cried,
    "You gave the choice to me.
I'm tired of sun and home and all,
    So a mermaid I will be."
Then bitter, salt sea-drops they gave,
    From out a hollow shell;
And garlands fair upon her head,
    They laid, with song and spell.
A cloud arose, like sudden mist;
    And, when it passed, the child
Found herself, by drop and garland,
    Changed to a mermaid wild.
With timid haste she glided down
    Into the cold, cold sea;
And bid her playmates show her where
    Her future home would be.
Down deep into the ocean went
    The mermaids, one and all,
O'er many a wondrous hill and dale,
    Through many a coral hall.
The child's heart in the mermaid's form
    Beat fast with sudden fear;
For all was gloomy, strange, and dim
    Beneath the waters clear.
She missed the blessed air of heaven;
    She missed the cheerful light,
She feared the monsters weird, who looked
    From caverns dark as night;
Her food was now sea-apples cold,
    And bitter spray she drank;

Her bed was made on barren rocks,
　　Of sea-moss, rough and dank;
Strange creatures floated far and near,
　　Or crawled upon the sand;
And soon she longed with all her heart
　　For the green, summery land.
Here Bessie lived; but daily grew
　　More restless than before,
And sighed to be a child again,—
　　Safe on the pleasant shore.
She often rose up to the light,
　　A human voice to hear;
And look upon her happy home,—
　　That now seemed very dear.
And children, wandering on the sands,
　　Saw, rising from the sea,
A little hand that beckoned them,
　　As if imploringly.
They often saw a wistful face
　　Look through the spray and foam;
And heard a sobbing voice that cried,
　　"O mother! take me home."
So, drearily, poor Bessie lived,
　　Till to a merman old,
She one day went, when most forlorn,
　　And all her sorrow told.
"If you would find your happiness,"
　　The merman answering said,
"Forget yourself, and patiently
　　Cheer others' grief instead.
Watch well the lives of your two friends,
　　The simple difference see;

And you will need no other help,—
    No other spell from me."
Then Bessie watched with heedful eyes,
    Wondering more and more,
That she had never cared to mark
    That difference before;
For Silvertail, though fair to see,
    Was wilful, rude, and wild.
"Ah! yes," sighed Bessie, while she looked,
    "As I was, when a child."
She led an idle, selfish life,
    Darkened by discontent;
And left a shadow or a tear
    Behind, where'er she went.
But Goldfin, with her loving heart,
    So cheerful and serene,
Left smiles, kind words, and happy thoughts
    Wherever she had been.
No little fish but came to her
    To heal its wounded fin;
No monster grim but opened wide
    His cave to let her in.
The rough waves grew more mild to her,
    Though cruel to great ships;
The sea-gulls stooped in their wild flights,
    To kiss her smiling lips.
She helped the coral builders small
    To shape their little cells,
And in the diver's dangerous path
    Laid heaps of pearly shells;
She guided well the fisher-boats
    Through many a stormy gale,

And lured away the angry winds
    From many a tattered sail;
She scattered pebbles on the beach,
    And sea-weed on the sands,
To gladden children's longing eyes,
    And fill their little hands.
These things she did with patient care,
    Forgetful of herself,
Till in the sea she was more loved
    Than mermaid, sprite, or elf;
While all the joy to others given
    Came back unconsciously,
To cheer and brighten her own life,
    Wherever she might be.
"Ah! now I know why I am sad,"
    Cried Bessie, at the sight,
"When I am good, as Goldfin is,
    My heart will be as light."
And henceforth Bessie daily grew
    More cheerful and content:
In generous acts and friendly words
    Her happy days were spent.
No longer lonely seemed the sea,
    So full of friends it grew;
Nor longer gloomy, for the sun
    Shone through the waters blue.
No more she wept beside the shore,
    But floated daily there;
And hung gay garlands on the rocks,
    That once were brown and bare,
Softly singing, as she looked
    With dim eyes through the foam:

"When I have learned my lesson well,
    I may be taken home.
Till I can rule my heart aright,
    And conquer my own will,
I'll wait and work and hope and try.
    Dear mother, love me still."
As thus the little mermaid cried,
    There came a sudden gleam;
A cold drop fell upon her cheek,
    And chased away the dream.
With wondering eyes did Bessie gaze
    About on every side,—
The rocks whereon the mermaids sat
    Were covered by the tide;
The great waves, with a solemn sound,
    Came rolling slowly on;
The fresh winds played among her hair;
    And all the dream was gone.
But Bessie long remembered it:
    The lesson did not fail;
And all her life she followed well
    Goldfin, not Silvertail.

Faded Flowers

Faded flowers, faded flowers,
    They are all now left to cherish;
For the hopes and joys of my young life's spring
    I have seen so darkly perish.

Cold, ah, cold, in the lone, dark grave,
    My murdered love lies low,
And death alone can bring sure rest
    To this broken heart's deep woe.

Faded flowers, faded flowers,
    They are all now left to cherish;
For ah, his dear hand gathered them,
    And my love can never perish.

Here, Take This, with the Pure and Silver Streaking

Here, take this, with the pure and silver streaking,
    And wind it, Darling, round and round for me:
What is your Highness? Style scarce worth the speaking
    When thou dost look, I am as great as He.

To the First Robin

Welcome, welcome, little stranger,
Fear no harm, and fear no danger;
We are glad to see you here,
For you sing "Sweet Spring is near."

Now the white snow melts away;
Now the flowers blossom gay:
Come dear bird and build your nest,
For we love our robin best.

Softly Doth the Sun Descend

Softly doth the sun descend
　　　To his couch behind the hill,
Then, oh, then, I love to sit
　　　On mossy banks beside the rill.

The Blessed Day

What shall little children bring
    On Christmas Day, on Christmas Day?
What shall little children bring
    On Christmas Day in the morning?
This shall little children bring
    On Christmas Day, on Christmas Day;
Love and joy to Christ their king,
    On Christmas Day in the morning!

What shall little children sing
    On Christmas Day, on Christmas Day?
What shall little children sing
    On Christmas Day in the morning?
The grand old carols shall they sing
    On Christmas Day, on Christmas Day;
With all their hearts, their offerings bring
    On Christmas Day in the morning.

Mountain-Laurel

My bonnie flower, with truest joy
    Thy welcome face I see,
The world grows brighter to my eyes,
    And summer comes with thee.
My solitude now finds a friend,
    And after each hard day,

I in my mountain garden walk,
        To rest, or sing, or pray.

All down the rocky slope is spread
        Thy veil of rosy snow,
And in the valley by the brook,
        Thy deeper blossoms grow.
The barren wilderness grows fair,
        Such beauty dost thou give;
And human eyes and Nature's heart
        Rejoice that thou dost live.

Each year I wait thy coming, dear,
        Each year I love thee more,
For life grows hard, and much I need
        Thy honey for my store.
So, like a hungry bee, I sip
        Sweet lessons from thy cup,
And sitting at a flower's feet,
        My soul learns to look up.

No laurels shall I ever win,
        No splendid blossoms bear,
But gratefully receive and use
        God's blessed sun and air;
And, blooming where my lot is cast,
        Grow happy and content,
Making some barren spot more fair,
        For a humble life well spent.

Chevalita

Chevalita,
Pretty creter,
I do love her
Like a brother;
Just to ride
Is my delight,
For she does not
Kick or bite.

Oh, Lay Her in a Little Pit

Oh, lay her in a little pit,
With a marble stone to cover it;
And carve thereon a gruel spoon,
To show a "nuss" has died too soon.

The Nautilus

A Fairy Boat Song

Launch our boat from the yellow sand,
Say farewell to the blooming land,
Furl airy wings, fold the mantles blue,
Drink one last cup of honey dew;
For we must leave our fairy home
On a moonlight voyage through the foam.
      Spread the silken sail
      To the summer gale,
   Low singing across the sea;
      Float away, float away,
      Through foam and spray,
   As if o'er a flowery lea!

Oh! fear no storm nor cloudy frown,
Though mightier ships than ours go down:
Our helmsman laughs at the wildest gale,
As he drops anchor and furls his sail;
For He who guides the sparrow's wing,
Whose love upholds the frailest thing,
      Has given a spell,
      To protect the shell
   Through the waves' tumultuous flow,
      When tempest-tost,
      Unwrecked, unlost,
   It sinks to calmer depths below.

Watch, dear mates, by the fading light,
The mariner small who steers aright,

By compass and chart unseen, yet true,
And ferries over an elfin crew,
With tiny rudder and sail and oar,
Voyaging safely from shore to shore;
  While the mermaids fair,
   With their shining hair,
 Glide up from their ocean home.
   "Come away, come away!"
   The sea-sprites say,
 As they beckon through the foam.

O evening star! serene and still,
Guard us with magic care from ill!
O summer moon! like herald bright,
Guide us along thy path of light!
O friendly waves! bear on your breast
Elfin wanderers to their rest!
   See, how low and dim,
   On the ocean's rim,
 Lies the shore we left behind;
   Farewell! farewell!
   Let the echo swell,
 Bear it home on your wings, sweet wind!

To Anna

Sister, dear, when you are lonely,
　　Longing for your distant home,
And the images of loved ones
　　Warmly to your heart shall come,
Then, mid tender thoughts and fancies,
　　Let one fond voice say to thee,
"Ever when your heart is heavy,
　　Anna, dear, then think of me."

Think how we two have together
　　Journeyed onward day by day,
Joys and sorrows ever sharing,
　　While the swift years roll away.
Then may all the sunny hours
　　Of our youth rise up to thee,
And when your heart is light and happy,
　　Anna, dear, then think of me.

Where is Bennie?

The cowslips in the morning sun
    Unfold each yellow cup,
And watch and wait and whisper low,
    "Why isn't Bennie up?"
The robins hop along the path,
    Peep in, then fly away,
Others think they come for crumbs.
    I hear them chirping say,
        "Where is Bennie?"

We see no more about the house
    The little checkered tire;
Four chairs around the table stand,
    And none need be made higher.
The hatchet hangs against the wall,
    The whittlings are swept away;
The little barrow rolls no more,
    And the old house seems to say,
        "Where is Bennie?"

Down by the willows, green and cool,
    The little brook flows on;
But seems to murmur sadly now,
    For all the boats are gone.
Miss Puss sits blinking in the sun,
    Ready for games of play,
Or roams about from room to room,
    While her soft mew seems to say,
        "Where is Bennie?"

Under the lindens, far away,
    In a cradle warm and wide,
A baby laughs and kicks and crows,
    With a small boy at her side.
They frolic there in that soft nest,
    Two happy little birds;
And when we call, the youngest sings,
    In a sweet song without words,
        "Here is Bennie."

Little Paul

Cheerful voices by the sea-side
Echoed through the summer air,
Happy children, fresh and rosy,
Sang and sported freely there,
Often turning friendly glances,
Where, neglectful of them all,
On his bed among the gray rocks,
Mused the pale child, little Paul.

For he never joined their pastimes,
Never danced upon the sand,
Only smiled upon them kindly,
Only waved his wasted hand.
Many a treasured gift they bore him,
Best beloved among them all.
Many a childish heart grieved sadly,

Thinking of poor little Paul.
But while Florence was beside him,
While her face above him bent,
While her dear voice sounded near him,
He was happy and content;
Watching ever the great billows,
Listening to their ceaseless fall,
For they brought a pleasant music
To the ear of little Paul.

"Sister Floy," the pale child whispered,
"What is that the blue waves say?
What strange message are they bringing
From that shore so far away?
Who is dwelling in that country
Whence a low voice seems to call
Softly, through the dash of waters,
'Come away, my little Paul'?"

But sad Florence could not answer,
Though her dim eyes tenderly
Watched the wistful face, that ever
Gazed across the restless sea,
While the sunshine like a blessing
On his bright hair seemed to fall,
And the winds grew more caressing,
As they kissed frail little Paul.

Ere long, paler and more wasted,
On another bed he lay,
Where the city's din and discord
Echoed round him day by day;

While the voice that to his spirit
By the sea-side seemed to call,
Sounded with its tender music
Very near to little Paul.

As the deep tones of the ocean
Linger in the frailest shell,
So the lonely sea-side musings
In his memory seemed to dwell.
And he talked of golden waters
Rippling on his chamber wall,
While their melody in fancy
Cheered the heart of little Paul.

Clinging fast to faithful Florence,
Murmuring faintly night and day,
Of the swift and darksome river
Bearing him so far away,
Toward a shore whose blessed sunshine
Seemed most radiantly to fall
On a beautiful mild spirit,
Waiting there for little Paul.

So the tide of life ebbed slowly,
Till the last wave died away,
And nothing but the fragile wreck
On the sister's bosom lay.
And from out death's solemn waters,
Lifted high above them all,
In her arms the spirit mother
Bore the soul of little Paul.

Philosophers Sit in their Sylvan Hall

Philosophers sit in their sylvan hall
And talk of the duties of man,
Of Chaos and Cosmos, Hegel and Kant,
With Oversoul well in the van;
All on their hobbies they amble away,
And a terrible dust they make;
Disciples devout both gaze and adore,
As daily they listen and bake!

To Conduce to My Own and Parents' Good

To conduce to my own and parents' good,
    Was why I left my home;
To make their cares and burdens less,
    And try to help them some.
'Twas my own choice to earn them cash,
    And get them free from debt;
Before that I am twenty-one
    It shall be done, I bet.
My parents they have done for me
    What I for them can never do,
So if I serve them all I may,
    Sure God will help me through.
My chief delight, therefore, shall be
    To earn them all I can,

Not only now, but when that I
    At last am my own man.

Wishes

"What shall we wish for?"
    The Children say,
As they wait and long
    For New Year's Day.
Oh, wish, little friends,
    For gifts that last,
When toys are broken,
    And bon-bons past.
Wish for cheerful hearts,
    And willing feet;
Wish for gentle tongues,
    And tempers sweet;
Wish for these, and find,
    When months have rolled,
A happy New Year
    Born of the Old.

My Beth

Sitting patient in the shadow
    Till the blessed light shall come,
A serene and saintly presence
    Sanctifies our troubled home.
Earthly joys, and hopes, and sorrows
    Break like ripples on the strand
Of the deep and solemn river
    Where her willing feet now stand.

Oh, my sister, passing from me,
    Out of human care and strife,
Leave me, as a gift, those virtues
    Which have beautified your life!
Dear, bequeath me that great patience
    Which has power to sustain
A cheerful, uncomplaining spirit
    In its prison-house of pain.

Give me, for I need it sorely,
    Of that courage, wise and sweet,
Which has made the path of duty
    Green beneath your willing feet.
Give me that unselfish nature,
    That with charity divine
Can pardon wrong for love's dear sake—
    Meek heart, forgive me mine!

Thus our parting daily loseth
    Something of its bitter pain,
And while learning this hard lesson,

My great loss becomes my gain.
For the touch of grief will render
     My wild nature more serene,
Give to life new aspirations—
     And new trust in the unseen.

Henceforth, safe across the river,
     I shall see for evermore
A beloved, household spirit
     Waiting for me on the shore.
Hope and faith, born of my sorrow,
     Guardian angels shall become,
And the sister gone before me
     By their hands shall lead me home.

Oh, the Beautiful Old Story

Oh, the beautiful old story!
Of the little child that lay
In a manger on that morning,
When the stars sang in the day;
When the happy shepherds kneeling,
As before a holy shrine,
Blessed God and the tender mother
For a life that was divine.

Oh, the pleasant, peaceful story!
Of the youth who grew so fair,
In his father's humble dwelling,
Poverty and toil to share,
Till around him, in the temple,
Marvelling, the old men stood,
As through his wise innocency
Shone the meek boy's angelhood.

Oh, the wonderful, true story!
Of the messenger from God,
Who among the poor and lowly,
Bravely and devoutly trod,
Working miracles of mercy,
Preaching peace, rebuking strife,
Blessing all the little children,
Lifting up the dead to life.

Oh, the sad and solemn story!
Of the cross, the crown, the spear,
Of the pardon, pain, and glory

That have made his name so dear.
His example let us follow,
Fearless, faithful to the end,
Walking in the sacred footsteps
Of our Brother, Master, Friend.

To Mother

I hope that soon, dear mother,
    You and I may be
In the quiet room my fancy
    Has so often made for thee,—

The pleasant, sunny chamber,
    The cushioned easy-chair,
The book laid for your reading,
    The vase of flowers fair;

The desk beside the window
    Where the sun shines warm and bright:
And there in ease and quiet
    The promised book you write;

While I sit close beside you,
    Content at last to see
That you can rest, dear mother,
    And I can cherish thee.

Peep! Peep! Peep!

Oh! merry is the life
    Of a beach-bird free,
Dwelling by the side
    Of the sounding sea,—
Where the little children
    Chase us as we go;
Where the pretty shells
    Murmur sweet and low;
Where the old folk sit,
    Basking in the sun;
Where the fisher-folk
    Rest when work is done.
"Peep! Peep! Peep!" we say,
    Tripping to and fro
On the pebbly shore,
    Where the ripples flow.

Oh! merry is the life
    Of a beach-bird free,
Building our nests
    By the sounding sea,
Seeking daily food,
    And feeding with care
The dear little ones
    Safely hidden there,
Teaching them to fly
    Boldly o'er the sea,—
On the weak wings they
    Flutter timidly.
"Peep! Peep! Peep!" we say,

Brooding there on high,—
Sea-weed beneath us,
   Above us the sky.

Oh! happy is the life
   Of a beach-bird free,
Playing our blithe games
   By the sounding sea.
High o'er the billows,
   In gay flocks we sail,
Kissed by the cool spray,
   Ruffled by the gale,
Watching the great ships
   As onward they glide,
Like white-winged birds,
   O'er the restless tide.
"Peep! Peep! Peep!" we say,
   Dancing in the sun,
Where no harm can reach
   From storm, dog, or gun.

Oh! merry is the life
   Of a beach-bird free;
Few griefs molest us
   By the sounding sea.
If rude winds destroy
   Our nests built with care,
Patiently we work
   The loss to repair;
If chilled by the gust,
   Or wet by the rain,
We do not fret, but

Wait for sun again.
"Peep! Peep! Peep!" we say,
　　Where'er we may be;
Which means, little child,
　　"Hurrah for the sea!"

* * *

A Lament for S. B. Pat Paw

We mourn the loss of our little pet,
　　And sigh o'er her hapless fate,
For never more by the fire she'll sit,
　　Nor play by the old green gate.

The little grave where her infant sleeps
　　Is 'neath the chestnut tree.
But o'er her grave we may not weep,
　　We know not where it may be.

Her empty bed, her idle ball,
　　Will never see her more;
No gentle tap, no loving purr
　　Is heard at the parlor door.

Another cat comes after her mice,
　　A cat with a dirty face,
But she does not hunt as our darling did,
　　Nor play with her airy grace.

Her stealthy paws tread the very hall
    Where Snowball used to play,
But she only spits at the dogs our pet
    So gallantly drove away.

She is useful and mild, and does her best,
    But she is not fair to see,
And we cannot give her your place, dear,
    Nor worship her as we worship thee.

Morning Song of the Bees

Awake! Awake! for the earliest gleam
    Of golden sunlight shines
On the rippling waves, that brightly flow
    Beneath the flowering vines.
Awake! Awake! for the low, sweet chant
    Of the wild-birds' morning hymn
Comes floating by on the fragrant air,
    Through the forest cool and dim;
        Then spread each wing,
        And work, and sing,
Through the long, bright sunny hours;
        O'er the pleasant earth
        We journey forth,
For a day among the flowers.

Awake! Awake! for the summer wind
    Hath bidden the blossoms unclose,
Hath opened the violet's soft blue eye,
    And awakened the sleeping rose.
And lightly they wave on their slender stems
    Fragrant, and fresh, and fair,
Waiting for us, as we singing come
    To gather our honey-dew there.
        Then spread each wing,
        And work, and sing,
Through the long, bright sunny hours;
        O'er the pleasant earth
        We journey forth,
For a day among the flowers.

Bright Shines the Summer Sun

Thistledown in prison sings:

Bright shines the summer sun,
　　Soft is the summer air;
Gayly the wood-birds sing,
　　Flowers are blooming fair.

But, deep in the dark, cold rock,
　　Sadly I dwell,
Longing for thee, dear friend,
　　Lily-Bell! Lily-Bell!

Lily-Bell replies:

Through sunlight and summer air
　　I have sought for thee long,
Guided by birds and flowers,
　　And now by thy song.

Thistledown! Thistledown!
　　O'er hill and dell
Hither to comfort thee
　　Comes Lily-Bell.

"I Shine," Says the Sun

"I shine," says the sun,
    "To give the world light,"
"I glimmer," adds the moon,
    "To beautify the night."
"I ripple," says the brook,
    "I whisper," sighs the breeze,
"I patter," laughs the rain,
    "We rustle," call the trees
"We dance," nod the daisies,
    "I twinkle," shines the star,
"We sing," chant the birds,
    "How happy we all are!"
"I smile," cries the child,
    Gentle, good, and gay;
The sweetest thing of all,
    The sunshine of each day.

Song of the Brook

I am calling, I am calling,
    As I ripple, run, and sing,
Come up higher, come up higher,
    Come and find the fairy spring.
Who will listen, who will listen
    To the wonders I can tell,
Of a palace built of sunshine,
    Where the sweetest spirits dwell?—
Singing winds, and magic waters,
    Golden shadows, silver rain,
Spells that make the sad heart happy,
    Sleep that cures the deepest pain.
Cheeks that bloom like summer roses,
    Smiling lips and eyes that shine,
Come to those who climb the mountain,
    Find and taste the fairy wine.
I am calling, I am calling,
    As I ripple, run, and sing;
Who will listen, who will listen,
    To the story of the spring?

Go up higher, go up higher,
    Far beyond the waterfall.
Follow Echo up the mountain,
    She will answer to your call.
Bird and butterfly and blossom,
    All will help to show the way;
Lose no time, the day is going,
    Find the spring, dear little May.

With a Rose

That Bloomed on the Day of John Brown's Martyrdom

In the long silence of the night,
Nature's benignant power
Woke aspirations for the light
Within the folded flower.
Its presence and the gracious day
Made summer in the room,
While woman's eyes dropped tender dew
On the little rose in bloom.

Then blossomed forth a grander flower,
In the wilderness of wrong,
Untouched by Slavery's bitter frost,
A soul devout and strong.
God-watched, that century plant uprose,
Far shining through the gloom,
Filling a nation with the breath
Of a noble life in bloom.

A life so powerful in its truth,
A nature so complete,
It conquered ruler, judge and priest,
And held them at its feet.
Grim Death seemed proud to a soul
So beautifully given,
And the gallows only proved to him
A stepping-stone to heaven.

Each cheerful word, each valiant act,
So simple, so sublime,
Spoke to us through the reverent hush
Which sanctified that time.
That moment when the brave old man
Went so serenely forth,
With footsteps whose unfaltering tread
Re-echoed through the North.

The sword he wielded for the right
Turns to a victor's palm;
His memory sounds for evermore,
A spirit-stirring psalm.
No breath of shame can touch his shield,
Nor ages dim its shine;
Living, he made life beautiful,
Dying, made death divine.

No monument of quarried stone,
No eloquence of speech,
Can grave the lessons on the land
His martyrdom will teach.
No eulogy like his own words,
With hero-spirit rife,
"I truly serve the cause I love,
By yielding up my life."

Merry Christmas

In the rush of early morning,
    When the red burns through the gray,
And the wintry world lies waiting
    For the glory of the day,
Then we hear a fitful rustling
    Just without upon the stair,
See two small white phantoms coming,
    Catch the gleam of sunny hair.

Are they Christmas fairies stealing
    Rows of little socks to fill?
Are they angels floating hither
    With their message of good-will?
What sweet spell are these elves weaving,
    As like larks they chirp and sing?
Are these palms of peace from heaven
    That these lovely spirits bring?

Rosy feet upon the threshold,
    Eager faces peeping through,
With the first red ray of sunshine,
    Chanting cherubs come in view:
Mistletoe and gleaming holly,
    Symbols of a blessed day,
In their chubby hands they carry,
    Streaming all along the way.

Well we know them, never weary
    Of this innocent surprise;
Waiting, watching, listening always

With full hearts and tender eyes,
While our little household angels,
    White and golden in the sun,
Greet us with the sweet old welcome,—
    "Merry Christmas, every one!"

My Prayer

Courage and patience, these I ask,
    Dear Lord, in this my latest strait;
For hard I find my ten years' task,
    Learning to suffer and to wait.

Life seems so rich and grand a thing,
    So full of work for heart and brain,
It is a cross that I can bring
    No help, no offering, but pain.

The hard-earned harvest of these years
    I long to generously share;
The lessons learned with bitter tears
    To teach again with tender care;

To smooth the rough and thorny way
    Where other feet begin to tread;
To feed some hungry soul each day
    With sympathy's sustaining bread.

So beautiful such pleasures show,
    I long to make them mine;
To love and labor and to know
    The joy such living makes divine.

But if I may not, I will only ask
    Courage and patience for my fate,
And learn, dear Lord, thy latest task,—
    To suffer patiently and wait.

Song of the Sea-Shell

Child

Tell me, sea-shell, white and pearly,
What is it you ever say
In your voice so low and pleasant,
Sounding as if far away.
Are they songs you sing so sweetly,
Taught by mermaids long ago,
Or the echoes, faintly whispered,
Of the ocean's ceaseless flow?

Sea-Shell

Lying scattered on the sea-shore,
Washed by billows rolling there,
Many strange and pleasant stories
In our memories we bear.
Winds and waters rage around us,
And our hollow cells retain
Every echo, but repeated
In a softer, sweeter strain.
Thus unconsciously we murmur
In our voices small and low,
The grand music sounding near us
In the ocean's ebb and flow.
Songs of mermaids we can sing you,
Tales of winds and waters tell,
And melodies of spirits whisper,
For we love their music well.
Listen to this simple story,

Eager, wondering little child;
Yonder small waves sing it often
To the sea-shore lone and wild.
Far away 'mong lonely mountains
Dwelt a sparkling little rill;
Lovely flowers bloomed beside it
In the forest cool and still.
Gaily sang the wild birds near it
Through the pleasant summer hours,
And the little brook was happy
'Mong its friends the birds and flowers.
Till one breezy, sunny morning,
An idle fairy told the rill
How pleasant 'twas to wander freely
O'er the broad green earth at will.
Told it of soft verdant meadows
Bright with streams that rippled by,
Where fairest flowers forever bloomed
Beneath a cloudless sky.
Told it of the broad blue ocean
Where the sunbeams loved to lie,
Where the free fresh winds were blowing,
And great waves went rolling by.
Told it of the strange bright spirits
Dwelling in that far-off sea,
Floating through their coral bowers,
Singing ever joyfully.
Thus the foolish idle fairy
Told of things so fresh and fair,
That the little streamlet longed
To leave its home and hasten there.
So it left the quiet mountain

Where it once was glad to dwell,
Heeding not the weeping flowers
Nor the birds that sang farewell.
Thinking of the fairy's story
And the sights it soon should see,
Down the hillside went the streamlet
Rippling on by rock and tree.
On it passed, through valleys lonely
And through forests dark and wild,
Still it saw no pleasant meadows
Where the sunlight ever smiled.
So it wandered sadly onward,
Seeking for a fairer home,
Till it met a mountain torrent
In its robe of snow-white foam;
And the waves, as on they hurried,
Told the rill that they were going
Where the earth was bright and pleasant,
And their friends were gaily flowing.
"Join us, join us, ere we vanish,
Thou shalt share the home we seek.
Come with us, and we'll befriend thee,
For thou art alone and weak.
See us! how we freely wander
Down the rocks and far away;
Come and journey onward with us,
Little brook, oh come away!"
Thus the wild waves urged the streamlet,
As they rippled side by side.
But the flowers that bent above it
With soft warning voices cried,
"Go not with the mountain torrent,

Do not listen to its call,
Stay with us among the valleys
Lest some evil should befall.
We will cheer thy lonely hours
With our music soft and low,
While beneath our drooping flowers
Placidly thy waves may flow,
Listen to our friendly warning,
Be not idly led astray;
When too late thou wilt repent it;
Little streamlet, stay, oh stay!"
But the brook still listened only
To the wild waves' joyous call,
And it plunged amid the tumult
Of the dashing waterfall.
Then away through glen and valley
Swept the torrent and the rill,
Never more to ripple calmly
Through those valleys green and still.
On they rolled, down rock and hillside,
Till before them rose a wall.
"Ah, they think to take us captive,"
Cried the angry waterfall,
"But to tame a free-born torrent
Vain will all their efforts be.
Fear not, little streamlet, follow
And boldly leap the wall with me."
Fast and high the waters gathered,
And then, with a sullen sound,
Down they dashed—but on a mill-wheel
Turning ever slowly round.
Here, in darkness and in terror,

Tossed and tortured ceaselessly,
Long the captive waters struggled,
Vainly striving to be free.
Till at length from their dark prison
'Neath the pleasant light of day,
Now no longer pure and stainless,
Fast the dark waves fled away.
But they danced and foamed no longer,
Singing gaily their wild song,
Now they murmured of their sorrow,
As they sadly flowed along.
And the discontented streamlet
Grieved that it had ever come,
Longed now vainly for the quiet
Of its happy mountain home.
Many a shadow dimmed its brightness,
Many a dark stain on it fell,
And it thought now of the flowers,
Of their warning and farewell.
Meanwhile onward flowed the streamlet
Through the pathways dark as night,
Till 'mid a group of graceful trees
It gushed forth into the light.
And the wild stream, now a fountain,
In a carved urn came to dwell,
Making soft a pleasant music
As the cool waves rose and fell.
Little children played around it,
Listening to its gentle song,
Bright birds came to drink its waters,
Flowers gazed in it all day long.
But the waves still murmured sadly,

"Give us back our liberty,
We are journeying from the mountains
To the far-off summer sea.
Set us free, and let us wander
O'er the pleasant earth at will,
We can find no joy in dwelling
In this garden lone and still."
But their prayer was all unheeded,
For their voices low and clear,
Whispering softly, was the music
That the children loved to hear.
Vainly strove the birds to cheer it,
Vainly smiled the flowers around,
Still the plashing fountain murmured
With a softly mournful sound;
So it dwelt a lonely captive,
Till the carved urn crumbling fell.
Then it glided from the garden
Happier than words could tell.
And ere long 'mong verdant mountains
Where the cool winds rustled by,
And lovely flowers blooming dwelt
Beneath a cloudless sky,
Came the broad stream rippling softly,
As it swiftly flowed along
By drooping trees who bowed to hear
The blue waves' cheerful song.
Then the little streamlet whispered,
"I am happy, I am free.
Here I find all I have sought for,
Here my quiet home shall be,
Here I can forget my wanderings

And the troubles that befell.
I shall journey on no further,
Mountain torrent, fare thee well!"
But the great waves loudly answered,
"This is not the home we seek,
Thou must follow where we lead thee,
We are strong, and thou art weak.
Far off to the boundless ocean
We are swiftly bearing thee;
Thou hast joined us, and no power
Now can ever set thee free."
Wildly pled the poor lost streamlet
As the dark waves round it rolled,
"But for you I should have heeded
What the gentle flowers told.
I have suffered for my folly,
Bitterly do I repent;
Now my lost home seems most lovely,
For I've learned to be content.
Once you promised to befriend me,
Then bear me not so fast away
To the cold, dark, stormy ocean;
Cruel stream, oh let me stay!"
But the torrent would not listen;
Fast the blue waves rolled along,
Heedless of the flowers' beauty,
Or the wild birds' happy song.
On through meadow, field and valley,
Flowed the broad stream steadily,
Till it joined a noble river
Rolling calmly to the sea.
Then through cities vast and noisy,

And through deserts wild and lone,
While upon its peaceful bosom
Stately ships went sailing on,
Leaving far behind the mountains,
On it swept through plain and glade,
Bearing still the helpless streamlet,
Sad, repentant, and dismayed,
Till at length into the ocean,
Welcomed by its solemn roar,
Mountain stream and noble river
Joyfully their blue waves pour.
With one farewell look of sorrow
On the earth so green and fair,
Rolled the brook into the ocean
Mingling with the billows there.
Wildly sang the strong, fresh breezes,
As they flitted to and fro,
While the mermaids' strange soft voices
Sounded faintly far below.
But though dwelling in the wild sea,
'Mid its tumult, spray and foam,
Still the streamlet murmured sadly
Tender songs of its lost home,
Ever singing softly, lowly,
As its blue waves kissed the shore,
Till the sea-shells caught its music
Echoing it forever more.

Have No Fear

Have no fear,
Friends are here,
To help you on your way.
The mountain's breast
Will give you rest,
And we a feast, dear May.
Here at your feet
Is honey sweet,
And water fresh to sip.
Fruit I bring
On Blue-bird's wing,
And nuts sends merry Skip.
Rough and wild,
To you, dear child,
Seems the lonely mountain way;
But have no fear,
For friends are near,
To guard and guide, sweet May.

Up, Up, Little Maid

"Up, up, little maid;
    Day has begun.
Welcome with us
    Our father, the sun!"

sang the larks, as they rose from the grass and waked
    Betty with their sweet voices.

"Tweet, tweet, it is morning;
    Please get up, mamma.
Do bring us some breakfast,
    Our dearest papa,"

twittered the young wrens, with their mouths wide open.

"Click, clack, here's another day;
Stretch our wings and fly away
Over the wood and over the hills,
Seeking food for our babies' bills;"

and away went the storks with their long legs trailing out
    behind, while the little ones popped up their heads
    and stared at the sun.

"Cluck! cluck!
Here's good luck:
Old yellow-legs
Has laid two eggs,
All fresh and sweet,
For our girl to eat,"

cackled the gray hens, picking about the shed where the
cock stood crowing loudly.

"Coo! coo! coo!
Come, bathe in the dew;
For the rosy dawn shines
Through our beautiful pines.
So kiss, every one,
For a new day's begun,"

called the doves softly to one another as they billed and
cooed and tripped about on their little pink feet.

Bonnibelle

Bonnibelle! Bonnibelle!
Listen, listen, while we tell
A sweet secret all may know,
How a little child may grow
Like a happy wayside flower,
Warmed by sun, fed by shower,
Rocked by wind, loved by elf,
Quite forgetful of itself;
Full of honey for the bee,
Beautiful for all to see,
Nodding to the passers-by,
Smiling at the summer sky,
Sweetening all the balmy air,
Happy, innocent, and fair.
Flowers like these blossom may
In a palace garden gay;
Lilies tall or roses red,
For a royal hand or head.
But be they low, or be they high,
Under the soft leaves must lie
A true little heart of gold,
Never proud or hard or cold,
But brave and tender, just and free,
Whether it queen or beggar be;
Else its beauty is in vain,
And never will it bloom again.
This the secret we would tell,
Bonnibelle! Bonnibelle!

Lullaby

Now the day is done,
Now the shepherd sun
Drives his white flocks from the sky;
Now the flowers rest
On their mother's breast,
Hushed by her low lullaby.

Now the glowworms glance,
Now the fireflies dance,
Under fern-boughs green and high;
And the western breeze
To the forest trees
Chants a tuneful lullaby.

Now 'mid shadows deep
Falls blessèd sleep,
Like dew from the summer sky;
And the whole earth dreams,
In the moon's soft beams,
While night breathes a lullaby.

Now, birdlings, rest,
In your wind-rocked nest,
Unscared by the owl's shrill cry;
For with folded wings
Little Brier swings,
And singeth your lullaby.

My Kingdom

A little kingdom I possess
    Where thoughts and feelings dwell,
And very hard I find the task
    Of governing it well;
For passion tempts and troubles me,
    A wayward will misleads,
And selfishness its shadow casts
    On all my words and deeds.

How can I learn to rule myself,
    To be the child I should,
Honest and brave, nor ever tire
    Of trying to be good?
How can I keep a sunny soul
    To shine along life's way?
How can I tune my little heart
    To sweetly sing all day?

Dear Father, help me with the love
    that casteth out my fear;
Teach me to lean on thee, and feel
    That thou art very near,
That no temptation is unseen
    No childish grief too small,
Since thou, with patience infinite,
    Doth soothe and comfort all.

I do not ask for any crown
    But that which all may win
Nor seek to conquer any world

Except the one within.
Be thou my guide until I find,
    Led by a tender hand,
Thy happy kingdom in myself
    And dare to take command.

What Polly Found in Her Stocking

With the first pale glimmer,
    Of the morning red,
Polly woke delighted
    And flew out of bed.
To the door she hurried,
    Never stopped for clothes,
Though Jack Frost's cold fingers
    Nipt her little toes.
There it hung! the stocking,
    Long and blue and full;
Down it quickly tumbled
    With a hasty pull.
Back she capered, laughing,
    Happy little Polly;
For from out the stocking
    Stared a splendid dolly!
Next, what most she wanted,
    In a golden nut,
With a shining thimble,
    Scissors that would cut;

Then a book all pictures,
      "Children in the Wood."
And some scarlet mittens
      Like her scarlet hood.
Next a charming jump-rope,
      New and white and strong;
(Little Polly's stocking
      Though small was very long,)
In the heel she fumbled,
      "Something soft and warm,"
A rainbow ball of worsted
      Which could do no harm.
In the foot came bon-bons,
      In the toe a ring,
And some seeds of mignonette
      Ready for the spring.
There she sat at daylight
      Hugging close dear dolly;
Eating, looking, laughing,
      Happy little Polly!

Our Little Ghost

Oft, in the silence of the night,
 When the lonely moon rides high,
When wintry winds are whistling,
 And we hear the owl's shrill cry,
In the quiet, dusky chamber,
 By the flickering firelight,
Rising up between two sleepers,
 Comes a spirit all in white.

A winsome little ghost it is,
 Rosy-cheeked, and bright of eye;
With yellow curls all breaking loose
 From the small cap pushed awry.
Up it climbs among the pillows,
 For the "big dark" brings no dread,
And a baby's boundless fancy
 Makes a kingdom of a bed.

A fearless little ghost it is;
 Safe the night seems as the day;
The moon is but a gentle face,
 And the sighing winds are gay.
The solitude is full of friends,
 And the hour brings no regrets;
For, in this happy little soul,
 Shines a sun that never sets.

A merry little ghost it is,
 Dancing gayly by itself,
On the flowery counterpane,

Like a tricksy household elf;
Nodding to the fitful shadows,
    As they flicker on the wall;
Talking to familiar pictures,
    Mimicking the owl's shrill call.

A thoughtful little ghost it is;
    And, when lonely gambols tire,
With chubby hands on chubby knees,
    It sits winking at the fire.
Fancies innocent and lovely
    Shine before those baby-eyes,—
Endless fields of dandelions,
    Brooks, and birds, and butterflies.

A loving little ghost it is:
    When crept into its nest,
Its hand on father's shoulder laid,
    Its head on mother's breast,
It watches each familiar face,
    With a tranquil, trusting eye;
And, like a sleepy little bird,
    Sings its own soft lullaby.

Then those who feigned to sleep before,
    Lest baby play till dawn,
Wake and watch their folded flower—
    Little rose without a thorn.
And, in the silence of the night,
    The hearts that love it most
Pray tenderly above its sleep,
    "God bless our little ghost!"

The Lay of a Golden Goose

Long ago in a poultry yard
    One dull November morn,
Beneath a motherly soft wing
    A little goose was born.

Who straightway peeped out of the shell
    To view the world beyond,
Longing at once to sally forth
    And paddle in the pond.

"Oh! be not rash," her father said,
    A mild Socratic bird;
Her mother begged her not to stray
    With many a warning word.

But little goosey was perverse,
    And eagerly did cry,
"I've got a lovely pair of wings,
    Of course I ought to fly."

In vain parental cacklings,
    In vain the cold sky's frown,
Ambitious goosey tried to soar,
    But always tumbled down.

The farmyard jeered at her attempts,
    The peacocks screamed, "Oh fie!
You're only a domestic goose,
    So don't pretend to fly."

Great cock-a-doodle from his perch
    Crowed daily loud and clear,
"Stay in the puddle, foolish bird,
    That is your proper sphere."

The ducks and hens said, one and all,
    In gossip by the pool,
"Our children never play such pranks;
    My dear, that fowl's a fool."

The owls came out and flew about,
    Hooting above the rest,
"No useful egg was ever hatched
    From transcendental nest."

Good little goslings at their play
    And well-conducted chicks
Were taught to think poor goosey's flights
    Were naughty, ill-bred tricks.

They were content to swim and scratch,
    And not at all inclined
For any wild goose chase in search
    Of something undefined.

Hard times she had as one may guess,
    That young aspiring bird,
Who still from every fall arose
    Saddened but undeterred.

She knew she was no nightingale
    Yet spite of much abuse,

She longed to help and cheer the world,
    Although a plain gray goose.

She could not sing, she could not fly,
    Nor even walk, with grace,
And all the farmyard had declared
    A puddle was her place.

But something stronger than herself
    Would cry, "Go on, go on!
Remember, though an humble fowl,
    You're cousin to a swan."

So up and down poor goosey went,
    A busy, hopeful bird.
Searched many wide unfruitful fields,
    And many waters stirred.

At length she came unto a stream
    Most fertile of all Niles,
Where tuneful birds might soar and sing
    Among the leafy isles.

Here did she build a little nest
    Beside the waters still,
Where the parental goose could rest
    Unvexed by any bill.

And here she paused to smooth her plumes,
    Ruffled by many plagues;
When suddenly arose the cry,
    "This goose lays golden eggs."

At once the farmyard was agog;
    The ducks began to quack;
Prim Guinea fowls relenting called,
    "Come back, come back, come back."

Great chanticleer was pleased to give
    A patronizing crow,
And the contemptuous biddies clucked,
    "I wish my chicks did so."

The peacocks spread their shining tails,
    And cried in accents soft,
"We want to know you, gifted one,
    Come up and sit aloft."

Wise owls awoke and gravely said,
    With proudly swelling breasts,
"Rare birds have always been evoked
    From transcendental nests!"

News-hunting turkeys from afar
    Now ran with all thin legs
To gobble facts and fictions of
    The goose with golden eggs.

But best of all the little fowls
    Still playing on the shore,
Soft downy chicks and goslings gay,
    Chirped out, "Dear Goose, lay more."

But goosey all these weary years
    Had toiled like any ant,

And wearied out she now replied
      "My little dears, I can't.

"When I was starving, half this corn
      Had been of vital use,
Now I am surfeited with food
      Like any Strasbourg goose."

So to escape too many friends,
      Without uncivil strife,
She ran to the Atlantic pond
      And paddled for her life.

Soon up among the grand old Alps
      She found two blessed things,
The health she had so nearly lost,
      And rest for weary limbs.

But still across the briny deep
      Couched in most friendly words,
Came prayers for letters, tales, or verse
      From literary birds.

Whereat the renovated fowl
      With grateful thanks profuse,
Took from her wing a quill and wrote
      This lay of a Golden Goose.

The Rock and the Bubble

Oh! a bare, brown rock
    Stood up in the sea,
The waves at its feet
    Dancing merrily.

A little bubble
    Once came sailing by,
And thus to the rock
    Did it gayly cry,—

"Ho! clumsy brown stone,
    Quick, make way for me:
I'm the fairest thing
    That floats on the sea.

"See my rainbow-robe,
    See my crown of light,
My glittering form,
    So airy and bright.

"O'er the waters blue,
    I'm floating away,
To dance by the shore
    With the foam and spray.

"Now, make way, make way;
    For the waves are strong,
And their rippling feet
    Bear me fast along."

But the great rock stood
     Straight up in the sea:
It looked gravely down,
     And said pleasantly—

"Little friend, you must
     Go some other way;
For I have not stirred
     this many a long day.

"Great billows have dashed,
     And angry winds blown;
But my sturdy form
     Is not overthrown.

"Nothing can stir me
     In the air or sea;
Then, how can I move,
     Little friend, for thee?"

Then the waves all laughed
     In their voices sweet;
And the sea-birds looked,
     From their rocky seat,

At the bubble gay,
     Who angrily cried,
While its round cheek glowed
     With a foolish pride,—

"You *shall* move for me;
     And you shall not mock

At the words I say,
        You ugly, rough rock.

"Be silent, wild birds!
        Why stare you so?
Stop laughing, rude waves,
        And help me to go!

"For I am the queen
        Of the ocean here,
And this cruel stone
        Cannot make me fear."

Dashing fiercely up,
        With a scornful word,
Foolish Bubble broke;
        But Rock never stirred.

Then said the sea-birds,
        Sitting in their nests
To the little ones
        Leaning on their breasts,—

"Be not like Bubble,
        Headstrong, rude, and vain,
Seeking by violence
        Your object to gain;

"But be like the rock,
        Steadfast, true, and strong,
Yet cheerful and kind,
And firm against wrong.

"Heed, little birdlings,
    And wiser you'll be
For the lesson learned
    To-day by the sea."

The Moon is Up, Wake Lady, Wake!

The moon is up, wake, lady, wake!
My bark is moored on yonder lake.
The stars' soft eyes alone can see
My meeting, dear one, here with thee.

Wake, dearest, wake! Lean from thy bower,
The moonlight gleams on tree and flower.
The summer sky smiles soft above;
Look down on me, thou star of love!

When It Comes Night

When it comes night,
We put out the light.
Some blow with a puff,
Some turn down and snuff;

But neat folks prefer
A nice extinguisher.
So here I send you back
One to put on Mr. Jack.

Stormy Winter's Come at Last

The stormy winter's come at last,
　　With snow and rain and bitter blast;
Ponds and brooks are frozen o'er,
　　We cannot sail there any more.

The little birds are flown away
　　To warmer climes than ours;
They'll come no more till gentle May
　　Calls them back with flowers.

Oh, then the darling birds will sing
　　From their neat nests in the trees.
All creatures wake to welcome Spring,
　　And flowers dance in the breeze.

With patience wait till winter is o'er,
　　And all lovely things return;
Of every season try the more
　　Some knowledge or virtue to learn.

March, March, Mothers and Grand-mammas!

March, march, mothers and grand-mammas!
   Come from each home that stands in our border!
March, march, fathers and grand-papas!
   Now young America waits in good order!
     Here is a flower show,
     Grown under winter snow,
Ready for spring with her sunshine and showers;
     Here every blossom grows
     Shamrock, thistle and rose,
And fresh from our hillsides the Pilgrim's
     May flowers.

Here is the New World that yet shall be founded;
   Here are our Websters, our Sumners and Hales,
And here, with ambition by boat-racing bounded,
   Perhaps there may be a new Splitter of rails.
     Here are our future men,
     Here are John Browns again;
Here are young Phillipses eyeing our blunders,
     Yet may the river see
     Hunt, Hosmer, Flint and Lee
Stand to make Concord hills echo their thunders.

Here are the women who make no complaining,
   Dumb-bells and clubs chasing vapors away,
Queens of good health and good humor all reigning,
   Fairer and freer than we of to-day;
     Fullers with gifted eyes,
     Friendly Eliza Frys,
Nightingales born to give war a new glory;

Britomarts brave to ride
Thro' the world far and wide,
Righting all wrongs, as in Spenser's sweet story.

Come now from Barrett's mill, Bateman's blue water,
Nine Acre Corner, the Centre and all.
Come from the Factory, the North and East Quarter,
For here is a Union that never need fall,
Lads in your blithest moods,
Maids in your pretty snoods,
Come from all homes that stand in our border;
Concord shall many a day
Tell of the fair array
When young America met in good order.

Two Pair of Blue Hose

Two pair of blue hose,
For Johnny's white toes,
So Jack Frost can't freeze em,
Nor darned stockings tease em,
So pretty and neat
I hope the small feat
Will never go wrong,
But walk straight and strong,
The way father went.
We shall all be content
If the dear little son
Be a second good John.

To Father

A cloth on the table where dear Plato sits
By one of the Graces was spread
With the single request that he would not design
New patterns with ink or red.
And when he is soaring away in the clouds
I beg he'll remember and think
Though the "blackbirds" are fair his cloth will be fairer
For not being deluged with ink.
May plenty of pens and of quiet
To my dear pa forever be given
Till he has written such piles that when on the top
He can walk calmly on into Heaven.

Thoreau's Flute

We sighing said, "Our Pan is dead;
His pipe hangs mute beside the river;—
Around it wistful sunbeams quiver,
But Music's airy voice is fled.
Spring mourns as for untimely frost;
The bluebird chants a requiem;
The willow-blossom waits for him;—
The Genius of the wood is lost."

Then from the flute, untouched by hands,
There came a low, harmonious breath:
"For such as he there is no death;—
His life the eternal life commands;
Above man's aims his nature rose:
The wisdom of a just continent,
And turned to poetry Life's prose.

"Haunting the hills, the stream, the wild,
Swallow and aster, lake and pine,
To him grew human or divine,—
Fit mates for this large-hearted child.
Such homage Nature ne'er forgets,
And yearly on the coverlid
'Neath which her darling lieth hid
Will write his name in violets.

"To him no vain regrets belong
Whose soul, that finer instrument,
Gave to the world no poor lament,
But wood-notes ever sweet and strong.

O lonely friend! he still will be
A potent presence, though unseen,—
Steadfast, sagacious, and serene;
Seek not for him—he is with thee."

❧

Transfiguration

Mysterious death! who in a single hour
    Life's gold can so refine
    And by thy art divine
Change mortal weakness to immortal power!

Bending beneath the weight of eighty years
    Spent with the noble strife
    Of a victorious life
We watched her fading heavenward, through our
    tears.

But ere the sense of loss our hearts had wrung
    A miracle was wrought;
    And swift as happy thought
She lived again—brave, beautiful, and young.

Age, pain, and sorrow dropped the veils they wore
    And showed the tender eyes
    Of angels in disguise,
Whose discipline so patiently she bore.

The past years brought their harvest rich and fair;
    While memory and love,
    Together, fondly wove
A golden garland for the silver hair.

How could we mourn like those who are bereft,
    When every pang of grief
    Found balm for its relief
In counting up the treasures she had left?—

Faith that withstood the shocks of toil and time;
    Hope that defied despair;
    Patience that conquered care;
And loyalty, whose courage was sublime;

The great deep heart that was a home for all—
    Just, eloquent, and strong
    In protest against wrong;
Wide charity, that knew no sin, no fall;

The spartan spirit that made life so grand,
    Mating poor daily needs
    With high, heroic deeds,
That wrested happiness from Fate's hard hand.

We thought to weep, but sing for joy instead,
    Full of the grateful peace
    That follows her release;
For nothing but the weary dust lies dead.

Oh, noble woman! never more a queen
    Than in the laying down

Of sceptre and of crown
To win a greater kingdom, yet unseen;

Teaching us how to seek the highest goal,
   To earn the true success—
   To live, to love, to bless—
And make death proud to take a royal soul.

Sweet! Sweet!

Sweet! Sweet!
Come, come and eat.
Dear little girls
With yellow curls;
For here you'll find
Sweets to your mind.
On every tree
Sugar-plums you'll see;
In every dell
Grows the caramel.
Over every wall
Gum-drops fall;
Molasses flows
Where our river goes.
Under your feet
Lies sugar sweet;
Over your head
Grow almonds red.

Our lily and rose
Are not for the nose;
Our flowers we pluck
To eat or suck.
And, oh! what bliss
When two friends kiss,
For they honey sip
From lip to lip!
And all you meet,
In house or street,
At work or play,
Sweethearts are they.
So, little dear,
Pray feel no fear:
Go where you will;
Eat, eat your fill.
Here is a feast
From west to east;
And you can say,
Ere you go away,
"At last I stand
In dear Candy-land,
And no more can stuff;
For once I've enough."
Sweet! Sweet!
Tweet! Tweet!
Tweedle-dee!
Tweedle-dee!

Daisy and Wee

"Daisy and Wee,
　　Come here, and see
What a dainty feast is spread:
　　Down in the grass
　　Where fairies pass,
Here are berries ripe and red.

"All wet with dew,
　　They wait for you:
Come hither, and eat your fill,
　　While I gayly sing,
　　In my airy swing,
And the sun climbs up the hill."

To My Lady

There are no flowers in the fields,
　　No green leaves on the tree,
No columbines, no violets,
　　No sweet anemone.
So I have gathered from my pots
　　All that I have to fill
The basket that I hang to-night,
　　With heaps of love from Jill.

Little Nell

Gleaming through the silent church-yard,
Winter sunlight seemed to shed
Golden shadows like soft blessings
O'er a quiet little bed,

Where a pale face lay unheeding
Tender tears that o'er it fell;
No sorrow now could touch the heart
Of gentle little Nell.

Ah, with what silent patient strength
The frail form lying there
Had borne its heavy load of grief,
Of loneliness and care.

Now, earthly burdens were laid down,
And on the meek young face
There shone a holier loveliness
Than childhood's simple grace.

Beset with sorrow, pain and fear,
Tempted by want and sin,
With none to guide or counsel her
But the brave child-heart within.

Strong in her fearless, faithful love,
Devoted to the last,
Unfaltering through gloom and gleam
The little wanderer passed.

Hand in hand they journeyed on
Through pathways strange and wild,
The gray-haired, feeble, sin-bowed man
Led by the noble child.

So through the world's dark ways she passed,
Till o'er the church-yard sod,
To the quiet spot where they found rest,
Those little feet had trod.

To that last resting-place on earth
Kind voices bid her come,
There her long wanderings found an end,
And weary Nell a home.

A home whose light and joy she was,
Though on her spirit lay
A solemn sense of coming change,
That deepened day by day.

There in the church-yard, tenderly,
Through quiet summer hours,
Above the poor neglected graves
She planted fragrant flowers.

The dim aisles of the ruined church
Echoed the child's light tread,
And flickering sunbeams thro' the leaves
Shone on her as she read.

And here where a holy silence dwelt,
And golden shadows fell,

When Death's mild face had looked on her,
They laid dear happy Nell.

Long had she wandered o'er the earth,
One hand to the old man given,
By the other angels led her on
Up a sunlit path to Heaven.

Oh! "patient, loving, noble Nell,"
Like light from sunset skies,
The beauty of thy sinless life
Upon the dark world lies.

On thy sad story, gentle child,
Dim eyes will often dwell,
And loving hearts will cherish long
The memory of Nell.

My Doves

Opposite my chamber window,
On the sunny roof, at play,
High above the city's tumult,
Flocks of doves sit day by day.
Shining necks and snowy bosoms,
Little rosy, tripping feet,
Twinkling eyes and fluttering wings,
Cooing voices, low and sweet,—

Graceful games and friendly meetings,
Do I daily watch and see.
For these happy little neighbors
Always seem at peace to be.
On my window-ledge, to lure them,
Crumbs of bread I often strew,
And, behind the curtain hiding,
Watch them flutter to and fro.

Soon they cease to fear the giver,
Quick are they to feel my love,
And my alms are freely taken
By the shyest little dove.
In soft flight, they circle downward,
Peep in through the window-pane;
Stretch their gleaming necks to greet me,
Peck and coo, and come again.

Faithful little friends and neighbors,
For no wintry wind or rain,
Household cares or airy pastimes,

Can my loving birds restrain.
Other friends forget, or linger,
But each day I surely know
That my doves will come and leave here
Little footprints in the snow.

So, they teach me the sweet lesson,
That the humblest may give
Help and hope, and in so doing,
Learn the truth by which we live;
For the heart that freely scatters
Simple charities and loves,
Lures home content, and joy, and peace,
Like a soft-winged flock of doves.

Sweet, Sweet Days Are Passing

Sweet, sweet days are passing
O'er my happy home.
Passing on swift wings through the valley of life.
Cold are the days when winter comes again.
When my sweet days were passing at my happy home,
Sweet were the days on the rivulet's green brink;
Sweet were the days when I read my father's books;
Sweet were the winter days when bright fires are blazing.

Sweetest of Maidens, Oh, How Can I Tell

Sweetest of maidens, oh, how can I tell
    The love that transfigures the whole earth to me?
The longing that causes my bosom to swell,
    When I dream of a life all devoted to thee?

Tell the Dear Old Body

Tell the dear old body
    This day I cannot run,
For the pots are boiling over
    And the mutton isn't done.

Dear Grif

Dear Grif,
Here is a whiff
Of beautiful spring flowers;
The big red rose
Is for your nose,
As toward the sky it towers.
"Oh, do not frown
Upon this crown
Of green pinks and blue geranium
But think of me
When this you see,
And put it on your cranium."

Here's a Nut

Here's a nut, there's a nut;
Hide it quick away,
In a hole, under leaves,
To eat some winter day.
Acorns sweet are plenty,
We will have them all:
Skip and scamper lively
Till the last ones fall.

Rock a Bye, Babies

Rock a bye, babies,
    Your cradle hangs high;
Soft down your pillow,
    Your curtain the sky.
Father will feed you,
    While mother will sing,
And shelter our darlings
    With her warm wing.

Work, Neighbor, Work!

Work, neighbor, work!
    Do not stop to play;
Wander far and wide,
    Gather all you may.

We are never like
    Idle butterflies,
But like the busy bees,
    Industrious and wise.

To J. M. B.

Oh, were I a heliotrope,
    I would play poet,
And blow a breeze of fragrance
    To you; and none should know it.

Your form like the stately elm
    When Phoebus gilds the morning ray;
Your cheeks like the ocean bed
    That blooms a rose in May.

Your words are wise and bright,
    I bequeath them to you a legacy given;
And when your spirit takes its flight,
    May it bloom a flower in heaven.

My tongue in flattering language spoke,
    And sweeter silence never broke
in busiest street or loneliest glen.
    I take you with the flashes of my pen.

Consider the lilies, how they grow;
    They toil not, yet are fair,
Gems and flowers and Solomon's seal.
    The geranium of the world is J. M. Bhaer.

The Children's Song

The world lies fair about us, and a friendly sky above;
Our lives are full of sunshine, our homes are full of love;
Few cares or sorrows sadden the beauty of our day;
We gather simple pleasures like daisies by the way.

>   Oh! sing with cheery voices,
>   Like robins on the tree;
>   For little lads and lasses
>   As blithe of heart should be.

The village is our fairyland: its good men are our kings;
And wandering through its by-ways our busy minds find
  wings.
The school-room is our garden, and we the flowers there,
And kind hands tend and water us that we may blossom
  fair.

>   Oh! dance in airy circles,
>   Like fairies on the lee;
>   For little lads and lasses
>   As light of foot should be.

There's the Shepherd of the sheepfold; the Father of the
  vines;
The Hermit of blue Walden; the Poet of the pines;
And a Friend who comes among us, with counsels wise
  and mild
With snow upon his forehead, yet at heart a very child.

Oh! smile as smiles the river,
    Slow rippling to the sea;
For little lads and lasses
    As full of peace should be.

There's not a cloud in heaven but drops its silent dew;
No violet in the meadow but blesses with its blue;
No happy child in Concord who may not do its part
To make the great world better by innocence of heart.

Oh! blossom in the sunshine
    Beneath the village tree;
For little lads and lasses
    Are the fairest flowers we see.

To One Who Teaches Me

To one who teaches me
The sweetness and the beauty
Of doing faithfully
And cheerfully my duty.

Hello! Hello!

Hello! hello!
Come down below,—
It's lovely and cool
Out here in the pool;
On a lily-pad float
For a nice green boat.
Here we sit and sing
In a pleasant ring;
Or leap frog play,
In the jolliest way.
Our games have begun,
Come join in the fun.

Sunlight

It comes from its faraway home in the sky,
And it gladdens each heart, it brightens each eye,
It enters the casement, it enters the door,
A welcome guest to the wealthy and poor.

It peeps o'er the mountain, it smiles on the plain,
And the bright young flowers have awakened again
From their dewy repose; and the blue Summer air
Bears upward their fragrant burden of prayer.

It pierces the depths of the forest dense,
Dispelling the darkness and gloom from thence,
Arraying each tree in a vestment of green,
While its rivulets gleam with a silvery sheen.

The rippling sea has a sweeter sound
As the up-flashing spray glistens brightly around,
And the wild forest bird in his home 'mid the trees
Warbles rapturous lays as its glory he sees.

Thou sunlight of beauty! Thou beam from bright Heaven!
May the comfort and joy which thy presence has given.
Be the foretaste of far richer ones yet to come,
When we rest in the light of an eternal home.

The Mother Moon

The moon upon the wide sea
Placidly looks down,
Smiling with her mild face,
Though the ocean frown.
Clouds may dim her brightness,
But soon they pass away,
And she shines out, unaltered,
O'er the little waves at play.
So 'mid the storm or sunshine,
Wherever she may go,
Led on by her hidden power
The wild sea must plow.

As the tranquil evening moon
Looks on that restless sea,
So a mother's gentle face,
Little child, is watching thee.
Then banish every tempest,
Chase all your clouds away,
That smoothly and brightly
Your quiet heart may play.
Let cheerful looks and actions
Like shining ripples flow,
Following the mother's voice,
Singing as they go.

The Sanitary Fair

Under battle-flags stained and torn,
Lie gifts from loyal hearts and hands,
Eager to answer love's demands,
And labor even while they mourn.

There is no need to vaunt these wares,
Wrought by man, maid, widow, wife,
For those who ventured limb and life,
Followed by loving hopes and prayers.

Memories born of place and time,
Serve those who keep their holiday
In camp, or hospital, or fray,
Where rings for them no Christmas chime.

Surely there is no heart so cold,
It will not freely give its mite
To keep a noble charity alight,
Throughout the new year as the old.

Soon may we see a Union stand,
Strong in love, liberty and law;
See also in our costly war
God's sanitary for the land.

Quee, Quee!

Quee, quee!
Wait and see:
You were good to me;
So here I come,
From my little home,
To help you willingly.

The Weary Bird Mid Stormy Skies

The weary bird mid stormy skies,
Flies home to her quiet nest,
And 'mid the faithful ones she loves,
Finds shelter and sweet rest.

And thou, my heart, like to tired bird,
Hath found a peaceful home,
Where love's soft sunlight gently falls,
And sorrow cannot come.

The Idle Wind

Little Effie strolled beside the sea;
Indolent, listless, and sad was she;
For her morning tasks were all unsaid,
Her work undone, her books unread,
The rocky seat where she should have been
Busily working, was empty seen;
Her sewing was thrown on the yellow sand,
The needle awaiting her idle hand;
The winds were turning the leaves of her book,
Where bright little sunbeams stole to look.
A curious fly in her thimble sat,
And a wondering beach bird pecked at her hat;
But she was away on the pebbly shore,
Hearing the blue waves' solemn roar.
"Stay, busy breeze," at length she cried,
Weary of watching the coming tide;
"Will you not stay and sing to me,
For I'm lonely here beside the sea."
The kind breeze stayed its airy flight,
And played awhile 'mong her locks so bright,
While its fresh voice whispered low and clear
This fable and song in Effie's ear.

"A little wind once, weary of play,
On a fluttering vine leaf idly lay,
And watched the sunlight gleam and glow
On the brook's blue waves that rolled below,
Singing a soft and dreamy song
To the drooping ferns, as they flowed along.
Forest and field were fresh and fair,

And birds' gay songs rang out on the air,
Blooming and bright did the green earth lie
'Neath the golden smile of the summer sky.

"The idle wind rocking to and fro
Spied a fair little flower just below;
The delicate bloom on its leaves was pale,
Its frail stem bent to the softest gale.
While the grass blades grew so tall and green
Its graceful head could scarce be seen,
But it still looked up to the summer sky
With a smiling face and a cheerful eye,
And thus to the indolent breeze it cried,
As the vine leaf bent and moved at its side:

"'Ah Summer-wind, why wilt thou idle be,
When good in the world may be done by thee?
Why wilt thou waste each fair summer day,
'Mong the leaves asleep, 'mid the flowers at play?
I know thou art sad, for I hear thee sigh,
And thy once gay voice goes murmuring by.
Though weak thou art, 'tis in thy power
To do some kindly deed each hour,
Each living thing, though frail and small,
May add its share to the beauty of all.

"'Each rosy cloud, though it fade and die,
Gives a deeper glow to the sunset sky;
Each fluttering leaf on the forest tree
Makes it fairer, statelier yet to see;
Each bird with its song of careless mirth
Gives another note to the music of earth;

Each little star in the still blue heaven
Adds to the solemn light of even;
Each drop that falls, though small it be,
Swells the restless waves of the mighty sea.

"'All lend their perfume, music, and light,
That the beautiful earth may be fresh and
    bright.
Ah listen, Summer-wind, for even thou too
Hast a daily work in the world to do.
Then up and away, thou'lt be happier far
While doing thy share, like bird, bee, and star;
And if thou but faithfully bearest thy part,
Thou wilt win content and joy of heart.'

"As the flower ceased, it turned away,
And a deeper bloom on its soft leaves lay.
Then the wind bent down to kiss its cheek,
And said, 'Dear flower, I am small and weak,
But my task henceforth I will bravely do,
Nor forget thy words so kind and true;
And whatever happiness comes to me,
Little friend, I shall owe it all to thee.'

"Then away to its work flew the busy breeze,
It swept the dust from the green old trees,
It rippled the waves in their graceful flow,
It rang the lily-bells lightly and low,
To lull the elves as they sleeping lay
Hid 'mid the leaves from the light of day,
It rocked the birds in their nests on high,
It chased dark clouds from the summer sky,

It sang through the pine boughs green and dark,
And bore on its wings the soaring lark.

"When the frail flowers dead and faded lay,
It wafted their winged seeds away
To other homes, where they might bloom,
And bring new light to the forest's gloom.
To the wandering bees it brought sweet tales
Of gardens fair, and flowery vales,
And guided them on to those unknown dells,
To gather fresh sweets for their waxen cells;
And bore kind words from butterflies gay
To lonely flowers dwelling far away.

"Among crowded homes it took its way,
Cooling the heat of the summer day,
Bearing fresh odors from distant hills,
Murmuring glad songs of birds and rills,
Kissing pale cheeks, lightly lifting soft hair,
Till smiling lips blessed the welcome air;
Through prison bars its cool breath swept,
Drying the tears of those who wept,
While its soft voice, sounding low and clear,
Woke tender thoughts to calm and cheer.

"So over the earth flew the tireless wind,
Leaving grateful happy hearts behind;
No longer it wasted the pleasant hours
In idle play 'mong the leaves and flowers;
No longer asleep in the vines it lay,
Lulled by the waves as they rolled away;
Now it labored with sunbeam, bird, and bee,

And made life sweet by its industry;
Till at last this idle little wind, it grew
The happiest, busiest breeze that blew."

The sea wind passed, and said no more;
But Effie silently left the shore,
Resolved to be happy, and more content,
Back to the rocky seat she went.
The beach bird flew away from her hat,
The fly in her thimble no longer sat,
The sunbeams turned their warmest look
On the earnest face bent over the book,
And the sea airs turned the leaves with care
For the busy child who now sat there.
A willing mind made the hard tasks light,
When to and fro glanced the needle bright;
The distant waves like echoes rang
To her cheery voice, as Effie sang:
"Like sunbeam, bird, breeze and bee,
I will make life sweet by industry."

To Papa

In high Olympus' sacred shade
    A gift Minerva wrought
For her beloved philosopher
    Immersed in deepest thought.

A shield to guard his aged breast
    With its enchanted mesh
When he his nectar and ambrosia took
    To strengthen and refresh.

Long may he live to use the life
    The hidden goddess gave,
To keep unspotted to the end
    The gentle, just, and brave.

Song of the Queer Green Frog

No, no, come and fly
Through the sunny sky,
Or honey sip
From the rose's lip,
Or dance in the air,
Like spirits fair.
Come away, come away;
'Tis our holiday.

The Blind Lark's Song

We are sitting in the shadow
  Of a long and lonely night,
Waiting till some gentle angel
  Comes to lead us to the light;
For we know there is a magic
  That can give eyes to the blind.
Oh, well-filled hands, be generous!
  Oh, pitying hearts, be kind!

Help stumbling feet that wander
  To find the upward way;
Teach hands that now lie idle
  The joys of work and play.
Let pity, love, and patience
  Our tender teachers be,
That though the eyes be blinded,
  The little souls may see.

Your world is large and beautiful,
  Our prison dim and small;
We stand and wait, imploring,
  "Is there not room for all?
Give us our children's garden,
  Where we may safely bloom,
Forgetting in God's sunshine
  Our lot of grief and gloom."

A little voice comes singing;
  Oh, listen to its song!
A little child is pleading

For those who suffer wrong.
Grant them the patient magic
That gives eyes to the blind!
Oh, well-filled hands, be generous!
Oh, pitying hearts, be kind!

O Lion, Grand

O lion, grand,
Come over the sand,
And help me now, I pray!
Here 's a little lass,
Who wants to pass;
Please carry her on her way.

To Poor Country Folks

To poor country folks
Who haven't any clothes
Rich folks, to relieve them,
Send old lace gowns and satin bows.

The Downward Road

Two Yankee maids of simple mien,
    And earnest, high endeavor,
Come sailing to the land of France,
    To escape the winter weather.
When first they reached that vicious shore
    They scorned the native ways,
Refused to eat the native grub,
    Or ride in native shays.
"Oh, for the puddings of our home!
    Oh, for some simple food!
These horrid, greasy, unknown things,
    How can you think them good?"
Thus to Amanda did they say,
    An uncomplaining maid,
Who ate in peace and answered not
    Until one day they said—
"How *can* you eat this garbage vile
    Against all nature's laws?
How *can* you eat your nails in points,
    Until they look like claws?"
Then patiently Amanda said,
    "My loves, just wait a while,
The time will come you will not think
    The nails or victuals vile."
A month has passed, and now we see
    That prophecy fulfilled;
The ardor of those carping maids
    Is most completely chilled.
Matilda was the first to fall,
    Lured by the dark gossoon,

In awful dishes one by one
    She dipped her timid spoon.
She promised for one little week
    To let her nails grow long,
But added in a saving clause
    She thought it very wrong.
Thus did she take the fatal plunge,
    Did compromise with sin,
Then all was lost; from that day forth
    French ways were sure to win.
Lavinia followed in her train,
    And ran the self-same road,
Ate sweet-bread first, then chopped-up brains,
    Eels, mushrooms, pickled toad.
She cries, "How flat the home *cuisine*
    After this luscious food!
Puddings and brutal joints of meat,
    That once we fancied good!"
And now in all their leisure hours
    One resource never fails,
Morning and noon and night they sit
    And polish up their nails.
Then if in one short fatal month
    A change like this appears,
Oh, what will be the next result
    When they have stayed for years?

Rosy, My Dear

Rosy, my dear,
Don't cry,—I'm here
To help you all I can.
I'm only a fly,
But you'll see that I
Will keep my word like a man.

Splash, Dash!

Splash, dash!
Rumble and crash!
Here come the beavers gay;
See what they do,
Rosy, for you,
Because you helped *me* one day.

The Flower's Lesson

There grew a fragrant rose-tree where the brook flows,
With two little tender buds, and one full rose;
When the sun went down to his bed in the west,
The little buds leaned on the rose-mother's breast,
While the bright eyed stars their long watch kept,
And the flowers of the valley in their green cradles slept;
Then silently in odors they communed with each other,
The two little buds on the bosom of their mother.
"O sister," said the little one, as she gazed at the sky,
"I wish that the Dew Elves, as they wander lightly by,
Would bring me a star; for they never grow dim,
And the Father does not need them to burn round him.
The shining drops of dew the Elves bring each day
And place in my bosom, so soon pass away;
But a star would glitter brightly through the long summer
    hours,
And I should be fairer than all my sister flowers.
That were better far than the dew-drops that fall
On the high and the low, and come alike to all.
I would be fair and stately, with a bright star to shine
And give a queenly air to this crimson robe of mine."
And proudly she cried, "These fire-flies shall be
My jewels, since the stars can never come to me."
Just then a tiny dew-drop that hung o'er the dell
On the breast of the bud like a soft star fell;
But impatiently she flung it away from her leaf,
And it fell on her mother like a tear of grief,
While she folded to her breast, with wilful pride,
A glittering fire-fly that hung by her side.
"Heed," said the mother rose, "daughter mine,

Why shouldst thou seek for beauty not thine?
The Father hath made thee what thou now art;
And what he most loveth is a sweet, pure heart.
Then why dost thou take with such discontent
The loving gift which he to thee hath sent?
For the cool fresh dew will render thee far
More lovely and sweet than the brightest star;
They were made for Heaven, and can never come to shine
Like the fire-fly thou hast in that foolish breast of thine.
O my foolish little bud, do listen to thy mother;
Care only for true beauty, and seek for no other.
There will be grief and trouble in that wilful little heart;
Unfold thy leaves, my daughter, and let the fly depart."
But the proud little bud would have her own will,
And folded the fire-fly more closely still;
Till the struggling insect tore open the vest
Of purple and green, that covered her breast.
When the sun came up, she saw with grief
The blooming of her sister bud leaf by leaf.
While she, once as fair and bright as the rest,
Hung her weary head down on her wounded breast.
Bright grew the sunshine, and the soft summer air
Was filled with the music of flowers singing there;
But faint grew the little bud with thirst and pain,
And longed for the cool dew; but now't was in vain.
Then bitterly she wept for her folly and pride,
As drooping she stood by her fair sister's side.
Then the rose mother leaned the weary little head
On her bosom to rest, and tenderly she said:
"Thou hast learned, my little bud, that, whatever may
    betide,
Thou canst win thyself no joy by passion or by pride.

The loving Father sends the sunshine and the shower,
That thou mayst become a perfect little flower;—
The sweet dews to feed thee, the soft wind to cheer,
And the earth as a pleasant home, while thou art dwelling
here.
Then shouldst thou not be grateful for all this kindly care,
And strive to keep thyself most innocent and fair?
Then seek, my little blossom, to win humility;
Be fair without, be pure within, and thou wilt happy be.
So when the quiet Autumn of thy fragrant life shall come,
Thou mayst pass away, to bloom in the Flower Spirits'
home."
Then from the mother's breast, where it still lay hid,
Into the fading bud the dew-drop gently slid;
Stronger grew the little form, and happy tears fell,
As the dew did its silent work, and the bud grew well,
While the gentle rose leaned, with motherly pride,
O'er the fair little ones that bloomed at her side.

Night came again, and the fire-flies flew;
But the bud let them pass, and drank of the dew;
While the soft stars shone, from the still summer heaven,
On the happy little flower that had learned the lesson
given.

They Come at My Call

They come at my call;
And though they are small,
They'll dig the passage clear:
I never forget;
We'll save them yet,
For love of Rosy dear.

Song of the Fly

Don't drive me away,
But hear what I say:
Bad men want the gold;
They will steal it to-night,
And you must take flight;
So be quiet and busy and bold.

Slip away with me,
And you will see
What a wise little thing am I;
For the road I show
No man can know,
Since it's up in the pathless sky.

The Water Spirits

Three little spirits sat in the sea
Under the shade of a red coral tree.
Graceful and high its branches spread,
Hung with bright moss overhead;
Soft was the sand and white as snow,
    Where many a gem was seen to glow;
    The blue waves rolled like a cloudless sky,
And strange bright things went gliding by;
But the spirits stood all silently
In the rosy shade of the coral tree.
"Seaweed," the eldest, was clad in green,
With a flowery crown and gems between.
She was slender and frail, and to and fro
Her light form bent with the waters' flow.
"Ripple," the next, was robed in blue,
Where a sunny light seemed shining through;
She was graceful and quick, and her voice was sweet,
And when at play no wave more fleet.
"Pearl," the youngest, was fair and pale;
Foam was her garment, and mist her veil;
She was gentle and kind, and all in the sea
Loved Pearl the best of the sisters three.
The Sea-King, their father, was lately dead,
And one of the three must reign in his stead.
They were fair and good, and the spirits all
Could not tell on whom the crown should fall.
So a council was held in the depths of the sea,
And a wise old sprite spake thus to the three:—
"Go, search far and wide through our ocean home,
Through cavern and cell fail not to roam,

And she who brings here the fairest thing
Shall wear the crown of our good old king.
Seaweed shall go to the far-off west,
And bear us thence the richest and best.
To the rosy east shall Ripple run,
And seek her gift toward the rising sun.
Pearl shall haste to the upper air,
And bring us down some treasure rare.
Till the full moon shines o'er the tranquil sea,
In your busy search ye may wander free;
But when her light o'er the waves is seen,
Then hasten back to choose the queen. "
All the spirits cried "So shall it be,"
And forth to their work went the sisters three.
When they'd said farewell 'neath the coral tree,
Seaweed went west, and long searched she
'Mid caverns and cells, damp, dark and low,
Hollowed in rocks by the waves' wild flow,
Where echoes strange through the arches rang,
And the winds' shrill voices loudly sang.
Here she gathered plants of many a hue,
Delicate seaweeds, green, orange, and blue,
Rare mosses that clung to the rocks so grey,
And made the waves with their colors gay.
All these she stored up, one by one,
Then with skillful hands a mantle spun.
Crimson and gold shone the border fair,
The rest was wrought with figures rare,
And fringed with floating seaweeds bright,
That lit the waves with their rainbow light.
"My work is not vain," said the spirit fair,
"'Tis a fitting robe for a queen to wear.

My task is done, I may idly roam
Till the full moon shines to call me home."
Ripple hastened away toward the rising sun,
And singing gaily, her task begun.
'Mid the wrecks of ships sunk deep in the sea,
The little sprite toiled busily
To gather the jewels scattered there,
And many she found most rich and rare.
Deep in the sand she sought them out,
And carefully searched the dells about,
Till a costly pile lay gleaming bright
Where the sunbeams shone, with softened light,
Through billows blue that arched on high
O'er the spirits' home, like a sunny sky.
Then Ripple toiled with magic skill,
And wrought the bright stones to her will;
With links of gold she bound them all,
And formed a graceful coronal.
Like a starry crown it glittering lay,
Each jewel shedding its brightest ray;
While the happy spirit gaily said,
"I shall seek no more, my gift is made,
With the winds and waves I will dance and play
Till the summer moon shall call me away."
Pearl floated up thro' spray and foam
Till far below lay her ocean home.
Long did she search, but all in vain,
She found no gift the crown to gain.
The time drew near, and she sought with speed
For some fair thing to help her need,
Like a snowflake over the waves she flew,
Till a green isle rose before her view;

Trees bent low to the murmuring sea,
And fresh winds rustled pleasantly,
Brilliant flowers with their odors sweet
Bent to the waves that kissed their feet,
And birds' glad voices echoed wide
To the melody of the whispering tide.
All these were fair to the spirit's eye,
Which seldom looked on earth or sky.
But fairer than bird or flowering spray
Was a little child on the shore at play,
Launching frail boats of leaf or shell,
With flowers or white foam laden well,
And laughing aloud in innocent glee,
As they floated or sunk in the sunny sea;
Chasing the beach birds, and bidding them stay
With winning voice, as they flitted away;
Catching bright bubbles with eager hand,
Or piling frail towers of yellow sand.
To the spirit's ear his childish words
Were sweeter far than the song of birds;
And she longed to be the summer air,
To kiss his cheek or play in his hair.
"We are pale and cold to this earth child bright,
And far less fair," sighed the water sprite;
"I would I could win him to go with me,
My gift would then the loveliest be.
I will seek no more, but linger here,
And seek to render myself most dear
By every art and spell in my power,
And bear him away at the given hour."
Then with music low on a hollow shell,
She danced on a wave as it rose and fell,

And with wooing words she softly smiled,
And beckoned away the wandering child,
Who watched her well in sweet surprise,
With joy and fear in his eager eyes.
Then she offered him sea flowers strange and rare,
And coral wreaths for his shining hair,
And sang soft melodies clear and wild,
Till she won the heart of the simple child.
Freely he took the gifts she bore,
Bidding her sing the gay songs o'er,
While he fearlessly dipped his little feet
In the waves she had rendered warm and sweet,
And hastened out thro' the gathering tide
To lie on a pillow of foam at her side,
While the winds with their music wild and free
Lulled him to sleep on the rocking sea.
Pearl knew not then that a mortal child
Would perish soon in her home so wild,
Or that loving hearts would sorrow long
If she lured him away with smile and song.
So she held him close, and laughed to see
How fair a gift he soon would be.
As she floated thus from the island shore,
A mournful voice, thro' the ocean's roar,
Fell on her ear, from the yellow sand,
Where she saw a weeping woman stand
With outstretched arms and accents wild,
Crying, "Oh give me back my child!
He cannot live in the great, cold sea,
Ah, spirit, lure him not from me!"
Silently Pearl heard the mournful cry,
And looked on the little one with a sigh,

Saying low to herself, "He is mine, I may go
With my beautiful gift to my home below.
I have sought in vain, 'twill be too late
For another search, and none will wait.
I shall never sit on my father's throne
If I give him back, and return alone
Without gift or treasure, to prove my right
To the royal crown and the sceptre bright.
Shall I do this thing so cruel and wrong,
Because he is weak and I am strong?
Ah no! let the crown and the kingdom go;
The voice of my own heart whispering low,
Will bring far greater joy to me
Than to rule as queen o'er the whole broad sea."
And whispering softly a fond farewell,
Still decked with sea flower, leaf, and shell,
She folded him tenderly to her breast,
And floated back on a great wave's crest;
And with murmured blessings low and sweet,
Laid the little child at his mother's feet,
Then vanished silently 'mid the foam
And journeyed away to her distant home.
In the high and arched halls of coral red
The spirits' welcoming feast was spread,
And joyful greetings echoed wide,
As the sisters three stood side by side.
Then Seaweed and Ripple proudly showed
The crown and mantle that brightly glowed,
And the spirits then with wonder cried,
"They are fit for a queen in all her pride;
And Pearl's gift must be fair indeed,
These lovely offerings to exceed."

Then Pearl, in a voice like a summer breeze,
Replied, "My gift was fairer than these;
A beautiful child, had I lured him down,
Had surely won for me the crown,
But a mother's tears I could not see,
So forgot myself, and set him free.
I can never reign, I know full well;
But a faithful subject I shall dwell,
And be happier far as a humble sprite
Than the proudest king, for my heart is light;
No bitter tears have been caused by me,
I am queen of myself, tho' not of the sea."
A murmur low thro' the spirit throng
Like a sudden wind, stole soft along;
And approving smiles on good Pearl fell,
Showing they loved and honored her well.
Her sisters turned to smile with the rest,
But Ripple cried, as she raised her vest,
"Ah, sister Pearl, by what magic power
Have you won for yourself this lovely flower?"
And lo! on her bosom blooming lay
A bud she had caught from the child in play;
Its crimson leaves were spread apart,
And odors stole from its golden heart,
So strange and sweet, the coral bowers
Seemed filled with the breath of earthly flowers.
And the spirits all with one voice cried,
As they drew more close to glad Pearl's side,
"This magic flower so fresh and fair,
That does not fade in the ocean air,
Is a richer, rarer gift in the sea,
Than crown or robe can ever be.

The power that saves the delicate rose
Is the love that deep in her own heart glows,
For even here in our home so wild
The bud has bloomed in the light of her smile;
Her gift is the fairest here ever seen,
And gentle Pearl is our chosen queen."

To My Father

On His 86th Birthday

Dear Pilgrim, waiting patiently,
    The long, long journey nearly done,
Beside the sacred stream that flows
    Clear shining in the western sun;
Look backward on the varied road
    Your steadfast feet have trod,
From youth to age, through weal and woe,
    Climbing forever nearer God.

Mountain and valley lie behind;
    The slough is crossed, the wicket passed;
Doubt and despair, sorrow and sin,
    Giant and fiend, conquered at last.
Neglect is changed to honor now;
    The heavy cross may be laid down;
The white head wins and wears at length
    The prophet's, not the martyr's crown.

Greatheart and Faithful gone before,
    Brave Christiana, Mercy sweet,
Are Shining Ones who stand and wait
    The weary wanderer to greet.
Patience and Love his handmaids are,
    And till time brings release,
Christian may rest in that bright room
    Whose windows open to the east.

The staff set by, the sandals off,
       Still pondering the precious scroll,
Serene and strong, he waits the call
       That frees and wings a happy soul.
Then, beautiful as when it lured
       The boy's aspiring eyes,
Before the pilgrim's longing sight
       Shall the Celestial City rise.

They Saw Again the Crocus Bloom

They saw again the crocus bloom,
And, leaning from that lofty room,
Sir Launcelot with face of gloom
       Look down to Camelot.
Up flew their veils and floated wide,
But Livy pinned them to her side,
"The curse has come upon us!" cried
       The ladies of Shalott.

The Jungfrau to Beth

God bless you, dear Queen Bess!
　　May nothing you dismay,
But health and peace and happiness
　　Be yours, this Christmas day.

Here's fruit to feed our busy bee,
　　And flowers for her nose.
Here's music for her pianee,
　　An afghan for her toes,

A portrait of Joanna, see,
　　By Raphael No. 2,
Who laboured with great industry
　　To make it fair and true.

Accept a ribbon red, I beg,
　　For Madam Purrer's tail,
And ice cream made by lovely Peg,
　　A Mont Blanc in a pail.

Their dearest love my makers laid
　　Within my breast of snow.
Accept it, and the Alpine maid,
　　From Laurie and from Jo.

Now Hark, Little May

Now hark, little May,
    If you want to do right,
Under your pillow
    Just look every night.
If you have been good
    All through the day,
A gift you will find,
    Useful or gay;
But if you have been
    Cross, selfish, or wild,
A bad thing will come
    For the naughty child.
So try, little dear,
    And soon you will see
How easy and sweet
    To grow good it will be.

Ha, ha! you can't see,
    Although I am here;
But listen to what
    I say in your ear.
Tell no one of this,
    Because, if you do,
My fun will be spoilt,
    And so will yours too.
But if you are good,
    And patient, and gay,
A real fairy will come
    To see little May.

Here Is the Bracelet

Here is the bracelet
    For good little May
To wear on her arm
    By night and by day.
When it shines like the sun,
    All's going well;
But when you are bad,
    A sharp prick will tell.
Farewell, little girl,
    For now we must part.
Make a fairy-box, dear,
    Of your own happy heart;
And take out for all
    Sweet gifts every day,
Till all the year round
    Is like beautiful May.

Who is the Fairest that Swims in Our River?

Who is the fairest that swims in our river?
    Who is the dearest frog under the sun?
Whose life is full of the sweetest endeavor?
    Who is our busiest, happiest one?
        Splash, Splash, darling thing!
        All delight her praise to sing.

Clover-Blossom

In a quiet, pleasant meadow,
    Beneath a summer sky,
Where green old trees their branches waved,
    And winds went singing by;
Where a little brook went rippling
    So musically low,
And passing clouds cast shadows
    On the waving grass below;
Where low, sweet notes of brooding birds
    Stole out on the fragrant air,
And golden sunlight shone undimmed
    On all most fresh and fair;—
There bloomed a lovely sisterhood
    Of happy little flowers,
Together in this pleasant home,
    Through quiet summer hours.
No rude hand came to gather them,
    No chilling winds to blight;
Warm sunbeams smiled on them by day,
    And soft dews fell at night.
So here, along the brook-side,
    Beneath the green old trees,
The flowers dwelt among their friends,
    The sunbeams and the breeze.

One morning, as the flowers awoke,
    Fragrant, and fresh, and fair,
A little worm came creeping by,
    And begged a shelter there.
"Ah! pity and love me," sighed the worm,

"I am lonely, poor, and weak;
A little spot for a resting-place,
    Dear flowers, is all I seek.
I am not fair, and have dwelt unloved
    By butterfly, bird, and bee.
They little knew that in this dark form
    Lay the beauty they yet may see.
Then let me lie in the deep green moss,
    And weave my little tomb,
And sleep my long, unbroken sleep
    Till Spring's first flowers come.
Then will I come in a fairer dress,
    And your gentle care repay
By the grateful love of the humble worm;
    Kind flowers, O let me stay!"
But the wild rose showed her little thorns,
    While her soft face glowed with pride;
The violet hid beneath the drooping ferns,
    And the daisy turned aside.
Little Houstonia scornfully laughed,
    As she danced on her slender stem;
While the cowslip bent to the rippling waves,
    And whispered the tale to them.
A blue-eyed grass looked down on the worm,
    As it silently turned away,
And cried, "Thou wilt harm our delicate leaves,
    And therefore thou canst not stay."
Then a sweet, soft voice, called out from far,
    "Come hither, poor worm, to me;
The sun lies warm in this quiet spot,
    And I'll share my home with thee."
The wondering flowers looked up to see

Who had offered the worm a home:
'Twas a clover-blossom, whose fluttering leaves
    Seemed beckoning him to come;
It dwelt in a sunny little nook,
    Where cool winds rustled by,
And murmuring bees and butterflies came,
    On the flower's breast to lie.
Down through the leaves the sunlight stole,
    And seemed to linger there,
As if it loved to brighten the home
    Of one so sweet and fair.
Its rosy face smiled kindly down,
    As the friendless worm drew near;
And its low voice, softly whispering, said
    "Poor thing, thou art welcome here;
Close at my side, in the soft green moss,
    Thou wilt find a quiet bed,
Where thou canst softly sleep till Spring,
    With my leaves above thee spread.
I pity and love thee, friendless worm,
    Though thou art not graceful or fair;
For many a dark, unlovely form,
    Hath a kind heart dwelling there;
No more o'er the green and pleasant earth,
    Lonely and poor, shalt thou roam,
For a loving friend hast thou found in me,
    And rest in my little home."
Then, deep in its quiet mossy bed,
    Sheltered from sun and shower,
The grateful worm spun its winter tomb,
    In the shadow of the flower.
And Clover guarded well its rest,

Till Autumn's leaves were sere,
Till all her sister flowers were gone,
    And her winter sleep drew near.
Then her withered leaves were softly spread
    O'er the sleeping worm below,
Ere the faithful little flower lay
    Beneath the winter snow.

Spring came again, and the flowers rose
    From their quiet winter graves,
And gayly danced on their slender stems,
    And sang with the rippling waves.
Softly the warm winds kissed their cheeks;
    Brightly the sunbeams fell,
As, one by one, they came again
    In their summer homes to dwell.
And little Clover bloomed once more,
    Rosy, and sweet, and fair,
And patiently watched by the mossy bed,
    For the worm still slumbered there.
Then her sister flowers scornfully cried,
    As they waved in the summer air,
"The ugly worm was friendless and poor;
    Little Clover, why shouldst thou care?
Then watch no more, nor dwell alone,
    Away from thy sister flowers;
Come, dance and feast, and spend with us
    These pleasant summer hours.
We pity thee, foolish little flower,
    To trust what the false worm said;
He will not come in a fairer dress,
    For he lies in the green moss dead."

But little Clover still watched on,
	Alone in her sunny home;
She did not doubt the poor worm's truth,
	And trusted he would come.

At last the small cell opened wide,
	And a glittering butterfly,
From out the moss, on golden wings,
	Soared up to the sunny sky.
Then the wondering flowers cried aloud,
	"Clover, thy watch was vain;
He only sought a shelter here,
	And never will come again."
And the unkind flowers danced for joy,
	When they saw him thus depart;
For the love of a beautiful butterfly
	Is dear to a flower's heart.
They feared he would stay in Clover's home,
	And her tender care repay;
So they danced for joy, when at last he rose
	And silently flew away.
Then little Clover bowed her head,
	While her soft tears fell like dew;
For her gentle heart was grieved, to find
	That her sisters' words were true,
And the insect she had watched so long
	When helpless, poor, and lone,
Thankless for all her faithful care,
	On his golden wings had flown.
But as she drooped, in silent grief,
	She heard little Daisy cry,
"O sisters, look! I see him now,

Afar in the sunny sky;
He is floating back from Cloud-Land now,
    Borne by the fragrant air.
Spread wide your leaves, that he may choose
    The flower he deems most fair."
Then the wild rose glowed with a deeper blush,
    As she proudly waved on her stem;
The Cowslip bent to the clear blue waves,
    And made her mirror of them.
Little Houstonia merrily danced,
    And spread her white leaves wide;
While Daisy whispered her joy and hope,
    As she stood by her gay friends' side.
Violet peeped from the tall green ferns,
    And lifted her soft blue eye
To watch the glittering form, that shone
    Afar in the summer sky.
They thought no more of the ugly worm,
    Who once had wakened their scorn;
But looked and longed for the butterfly now,
    As the soft wind bore him on.

Nearer and nearer the bright form came,
    And fairer the blossoms grew;
Each welcomed him, in her sweetest tones;
    Each offered her honey and dew.
But in vain did they beckon, and smile, and call,
    And wider their leaves unclose;
The glittering form still floated on,
    By Violet, Daisy, and Rose.
Lightly it flew to the pleasant home
    Of the flower most truly fair,

On Clover's breast he softly lit,
        And folded his bright wings there.
"Dear flower," the butterfly whispered low,
        "Long hast thou waited for me;
Now I am come, and my grateful love
        Shall brighten thy home for thee;
Thou hast loved and cared for me, when alone,
        Hast watched o'er me long and well;
And now will I strive to show the thanks
        The poor worm could not tell.
Sunbeam and breeze shall come to thee,
        And the coolest dews that fall;
Whate'er a flower can wish is thine,
        For thou art worthy all.
And the home thou shared with the friendless worm
        The butterfly's home shall be;
And thou shalt find, dear, faithful flower,
        A loving friend in me."
Then, through the long, bright summer hours
        Through sunshine and through shower,
Together in their happy home
        Dwelt butterfly and flower.

Not a Sparrow Falleth

Not a sparrow falleth but its God doth know,
Just as when his mandate lays a monarch low;
Not a leaflet moveth, but its God doth see,—
Think not, then, O mortal, God forgetteth thee.
Far more precious surely than the birds that fly
Is a Father's image to a Father's eye.
E'en thy hairs are numbered; trust Him full and free,
Cast thy cares before Him, He will comfort thee;
For the God that planted in thy breast a soul,
On his sacred tables doth thy name enroll.
Cheer thine heart, then, mortal, never faithless be,
He that marks the sparrows will remember thee.

Anniversary Ode

Again we meet to celebrate
    With badge and solemn rite,
Our fifty-second anniversary,
    In Pickwick Hall, tonight.

We all are here in perfect health,
    None gone from our small band:
Again we see each well-known face,
    And press each friendly hand.

Our Pickwick, always at his post,
    With reverence we greet,
As, spectacles on nose, he reads
    Our well-filled weekly sheet.

Although he suffers from a cold,
    We joy to hear him speak,
For words of wisdom from him fall,
    In spite of croak or squeak.

Old six-foot Snodgrass looms on high,
    With elephantine grace,
And beams upon the company,
    With brown and jovial face.

Poetic fire lights up his eye,
    He struggles 'gainst his lot.
Behold ambition on his brow,
    And on his nose, a blot.

Next our peaceful Tupman comes,
　　So rosy, plump, and sweet,
Who chokes with laughter at the puns,
　　And tumbles off his seat.

Prim little Winkle too is here,
　　With every hair in place,
A model of propriety,
　　Though he hates to wash his face.

The year is gone, we still unite
　　To joke and laugh and read,
And tread the path of literature
　　That doth to glory lead.

Long may our paper prosper well,
　　Our club unbroken be,
And coming years their blessings pour
　　On the useful, gay "P. C."

F. A. P.

Who likes to read a fairy tale,
Or stories told of sword and sail,
Until his little optics fail?
                Our boy.

Who loves his father's watch to wear
And often draw it out with care
Upon its round white face to stare?
                Our boy.

Who rather proud of his small feat
When wearing slippers new and neat,
And stockings red as any beet?
                Our boy.

Who in his pocket keep his hands
As round the house he "mooning" stands
Or reads the paper like the mans?
                Our boy.

Who likes to "boss" it over Jack,
And sometimes gives a naughty whack,
But gets it heartily paid back?
                Our boy.

Who likes to have a birthday frolic
And eats until he has a colic,
That for the time is diabolic?
                Our boy.

Who is the dearest little lad,
That aunt or mother ever had,
To love when gay and cheer when sad?
                    Our boy.

May angels guard him with their wings,
And all brave, good and happy things,
Make nobler thou than crowned kings.
                    Our boy.

The Prophecy

Trevlyn lands and Trevlyn gold,
Heir nor heiress e'er shall hold,
Undisturbed, till, spite of rust,
Truth is found in Trevlyn dust.

A Little Kettle

A little kettle, fat and fair,
    To sit on grandma's stove,
To simmer softly, and to sing
    A song of Freddie's love.

A Wail Uttered in the Woman's Club

God bless you, merry ladies,
    May nothing you dismay,
As you sit here at ease and hark
    Unto my dismal lay.
Get out your pocket-handkerchiefs,
    Give o'er your jokes and songs,
Forget awhile your Woman's Rights,
    And pity author's wrongs.

There is a town of high repute,
    Where saints and sages dwell,
Who in these latter days are forced
    To bid sweet peace farewell;
For all their men are demigods,—
    So rumor doth declare,—
And all the women are De Staels,
    And genius fills the air.

So eager pilgrims penetrate
    To their most private nooks,
Storm their back doors in search of news
    And interview their cooks,
Worship at every victim's shrine,
    See haloes round their hats,
Embalm the chickweed from their yards
    And photograph their cats.

There's Emerson, the poet wise,
    This much-enduring man,
Sees Jenkinses from every clime,

But dodges when he can.
Chaos and Cosmos down below
  Their waves of trouble roll,
While safely in his attic locked,
  He woos the Oversoul.

And Hawthorne, shy as any maid,
  From these invaders fled
Out of the window like a wraith,
  Or to his tower sped—
Till vanishing from this rude world,
  He left behind no clue,
Except along the hillside path
  The violet's tender blue.

Channing scarce dares at eventide
  To leave his lonely lair;
Reporters lurk on every side
  And hunt him like a bear.
Quaint Thoreau sought the wilderness,
  But callers by the score
Scared the poor hermit from his cell,
  The woodchuck from his door.

There's Alcott, the philosopher,
  Who labored long and well
Plato's Republic to restore,
  Now keeps a free hotel;
Whole boarding-schools of gushing girls
  The hapless mansion throng,
And Young Men's Christian U-ni-ons,
  Full five-and-seventy strong.

Alas! what can the poor souls do?
    Their homes are homes no more;
No washing-day is sacred now;
    Spring cleaning's never o'er.
Their doorsteps are the stranger's camp,
    Their trees bear many a name,
Artists their very nightcaps sketch;
    And this—and this, is fame!

Deluded world! your Mecca is
    A sand-bank glorified;
The river that you seek and sing
    Has "skeeters," but no tide.
The gods raise "garden-sarse and milk,"
    And in these classic shades
Dwell nineteen chronic invalids
    And forty-two old maids.

Some April shall the world behold
    Embattled authors stand,
With steel-pens of the sharpest tip
    In every inky hand.
Their bridge shall be a bridge of sighs,
    Their motto, "Privacy";
Their bullets like that Luther flung
    When bidding Satan flee.

Their monuments of ruined books,
    Of precious wasted days,
Of tempers tried, distracted brains,
    That might have won fresh bays.
And round this sad memorial,

Oh, chant for requiem:
Here lie our murdered geniuses;
    Concord has conquered them.

⚜

The Wild Birds Sing in the Orange Groves

The wild birds sing in the orange groves,
    And brightly bloom the flowers;
The fair earth smiles 'neath a summer sky
    Through the joyous fleeting hours.
But oh! in the slave girl's lonely heart,
    Sad thoughts and memories dwell,
And tears fall fast as she mournfully sings,
    Home, dear home, farewell!

Though the chains they bind be all of flowers,
    Where no hidden thorn may be,
Still the free heart sighs 'neath its fragrant bonds,
    And pines for its liberty.
And sweet, sad thoughts of the joy now gone,
    In the slave girl's heart shall dwell,
As she mournfully sings to her sighing harp,
    Native land, native land, farewell!

On This You Scratch

On this you scratch
Your little match.
When the spark flies
Look out for your eyes!
When the lucifer goes
Look out for your nose!
Little Jack gives you this
With a birthday kiss.

Within Doth Lie

Within doth lie
A silken tie,
Your dress to deck;
Soft and warm
As daughter's arm
Round mother's neck.

Dear Madam, With Respect

Dear madam, with respect
 My offering I bring;
The hooks all baited well,
 And ready for a spring.
No more the cunning mice
 Your biscuits shall abuse,
Nor put their babes to sleep
 Within your fur-lined shoes.
The trap my work must do;
 Forgive your portly cat,
For he, like you, has grown
 For lively work too fat.
All larger, fiercer game
 I gallantly defy,
And squirrel, rat and mole
 Beneath my paw shall die.
So, with this solemn vow,
 T. Pib his gift presents,
And sprawling at your feet
 Purrs forth his compliments.

Index of First Lines